VOYAGE

TO THE

CROSSROADS

CLASSIFIED CLASSIFIED CLASSIFIED CLASSIFIED CLASSIFIED

A YANKEE CREW TAKES YAMAMOTO'

VOYAGE

TO THE

CROSSROADS

LAST CRUISE OF THE BATTLESHIP *NAGATO*

FLAGSHIP TO THE ATOMIC TESTS AT BIKINI

VIC SOCOTRA

WITH

EDWARD SMITH GILFILLEN

SOCOTRA HOUSE PUBLICATIONS LLC

Culpeper, VA

Published by Socotra House Publishing LLC
Culpeper, VA
First printing 2016

Cover Photo: Imperial Japanese Navy via U.S. Navy

Cover and interior design by The Book Cover Whisperer:
OpenBookDesign.biz

978-1-63821-190-7 Paperback
978-1-63821-178-5 eBook

SECOND EDITION

This book is dedicated to the memory of Edward Smith Gilfillen, whose story should have been told long ago, and for all the Atomic Veterans whose lives were cut short due to exposure to radiation.

CONTENTS

ALPHA AND OMEGA

December 7, 2015, the 74th Anniversary of the attack on Pearl. It is always an emotional day for old sailors, particularly those who had the chance to serve in the very place where it occurred.

This year, I find myself attending to the Omega end of the attack - the last deployment of the battleship *Nagato*, whose powerful radio transmitters had received the three-word command to launch the assault on the still-sleeping island early on a lovely Sunday morning: "Tora! Tora! Tora!"

By the time the Alpha moment in the conflict had passed, there were 2,042 Americans killed and 1,247 wounded. The American Pacific Fleet was largely on the bottom of the shallow harbor, and *Nagato* and her carrier strike force - the Kido Butai - were retiring to the northwest.

It was the "18 *huge* radio tubes and a big variable condenser" from the radio room of the Japanese warship that brought me to the remarkable story of the Last Japanese Battleship, that and several exchanges with RADM Donald "Mac" Showers, last of the Station HYPO codebreakers, who had one of *Nagato's* battle flags for years. I will tell you how he came to have it, and why he decided to donate it to be displayed in the lobby of the Office of Naval Intelligence in Suitland, Maryland in a moment.

That would have been enough to pique my interest in *Nagato's* epic saga, but I was brought to her years ago by my Uncle Jim, who helped the widow of an Atomic Veteran get some other artifacts of the venerable battleship to the Antique Wireless Association's Museum (www.antiquewireless.org.) in Bloomfield, New York.

In the meantime, this was a day to remember the moment when America's innocence was lost amid a humiliating defeat. The great ships were still on the bottom when our pal ENS Mac Showers arrived in February of 1942, and the great struggle against the Empire of Japan was just beginning to unfold.

When I was in Pearl for the retirement of an old shipmate in early 2015, I was sitting on the pier under a white canvas awning, looking out across the placid waters toward the bookends at Ford Island.

Arizona slumbers beneath the soaring white arches of her memorial. She is the Alpha of the conflict. Just to her stern is the Omega, the vast gray bulk of the greatest battleship of them all, USS *Missouri* (BB-63), with the modest brass plaque on her deck that marks the very spot where the instrument of Japan's surrender was signed in 1945.

Remember Pearl Harbor.

BAKER'S DOZEN

"Warfare, perhaps civilization itself, has been brought to a turning point by this revolutionary weapon."

- VICE ADMIRAL W. H. P. BLANDY, USN,
COMMANDER OF OPERATION CROSSROADS

Combat Artist Grant Powers painted this striking image of USS Arkansas starting to go vertical into the BAKER water column. We watched in amazement from USS Mount McKinley (AGC-7), Flagship of Operation CROSSROADS underway. Photo Navy Historical and Heritage Command).

These Are the Words of Ed Gilfillen:

After we abandoned ship just as we had for the ABLE shot to get a safe distance from the coming atomic explosion. The pirate American crew was dispersed among the dozens of support ships. A dozen of us found ourselves on RADM Blandy's Joint Task Force ONE flagship, *Mount McKinley* (AGC-7), which was anchored about a dozen miles away from the target ships in the lagoon.

SECNAV James Forrestal himself was there, in plain unadorned khakis, along with congressmen and other Washington people interested in the new atomic technology. CROSSROADS was anything but secret, as opposed to the Manhattan Project that gave birth to the Bomb. These tests were intended to publicly demonstrate the might of this new technology to the world, and it certainly did that.

We jokingly called ourselves the BAKER'S DOZEN, since we expected to return to the mighty ex-IJN battleship *Nagato* once the test was complete. We would then try to clean the ship up from any fallout and begin preparations for the third in the series, blast CHARLIE. That one was planned to demonstrate the properties of an atomic explosion in deep water.

As it turns out, it did not happen that way, and like Test ABLE, there was a SNAFU that changed everything.

We rose early on the morning of the 25th of July and got chow in the wardroom before venturing out on deck to find a good perch to watch the test. We marveled at the VIP guests who were aboard to witness the event.

We were told that shot BAKER was expected to cause more damage to the target fleet than ABLE because it was an underwater detonation and closer to the surface. It was also expected to produce more radioactive contamination in Bikini Lagoon, although no one knew how *much* more. As it turned out, contamination from BAKER caused major problems that persisted for months and threatened the overall success of the entire CROSSROADS operation.

Pre-shot procedures were essentially the same as for ABLE: 68 target ships were moored in the lagoon and 24 small craft were beached on Bikini; all personnel were evacuated to the support fleet, which retreated upwind; and VIP observers and the press awaited the shot.

There was one important difference from the first test. This time we were encouraged to watch it directly. The scientists told us that since the blast was going to be at a depth of ninety feet, there would be no fireball, so we needed no goggles or smoked glasses.

We were on deck, looking toward the low dark silhouette of *LSM-60*, the heavily modified landing ship that lowered the bomb below the surface of the lagoon. The minutes clicked by, and we were advised over the ship's loudspeaker that preparations were complete and M-Hour would be at 0835. I checked my watch to best advantage and moved to the rail to get the best view I could.

The signal was broadcast to the mast over the landing ship as planned, and then things became very interesting.

An image of the initial water column, Nagato's distinctive pagoda mast is seen at lower right. Photo USN.

The scientists told us later that the underwater fireball generated by the blast took the form of a rapidly expanding hot gas bubble, which reached down to the sea floor and up to the surface simultaneously. The result created a shallow crater on the seafloor 30 feet deep and nearly 2,000 feet wide. At the top, water burst through the surface like a geyser, creating a massive "spray dome" containing nearly two million tons of highly radioactive seawater.

What we saw was a thing that resembled an angry cauliflower in rapid motion. The expanding dome stretched into a hollow chimney of spray called the "column," 6000 feet tall and 2000 feet wide, with walls 300 feet thick.

In one of the images I have in my copy of the pictorial history (H.M. Wise Co., 1946), there is a two-page depiction that includes a dark vertical shape at the base of the cauliflower. That was the USS *Arkansas* (BB-33), closest ship to the epicenter. The raw power of the BAKER device upended the 27,000-ton ship, thrusting its 562-feet hull stern first straight up in the air and then plunging the bow into the bottom of the lagoon before it toppled over backward into the water curtain of the spray column.

I could see *Nagato's* distinctive profile at the base of the column, and then it was obscured as the space vacated by the rising gas bubble caused a tsunami nearly a hundred feet tall. In some of the pictures the CROSSROADS historian published you can see *Nagato* completely immersed in it, though the old girl held her own and stayed afloat.

By the time the wave reached Bikini Island beach 3.5 miles away, a series of nine 15-foot waves tossed landing craft onto the strand and filled them with sand. Ten seconds after the detonation, falling water from the column created a 900-foot "base surge" which rolled over *Nagato* and the others, coating them with radioactivity so thoroughly that they could never be decontaminated. That was the SNAFU, maybe bigger than the one that landed the ABLE bomb so far off its intended target.

BAKER inflicted heavy damage on the target fleet. Eight ships, including the gallant aircraft carrier Saratoga (CV-3), were sunk; eight more were seriously damaged. Even more important for the remainder of the operation, the detonation caused most of the target fleet to be bathed in radioactive water spray and debris from the material dredged from the bottom of the lagoon.

The water in the lagoon near surface zero was intensely radioactive for several days as Admiral Blandy conferred with the scientists and tried to figure out what to do.

One thing I can say with certainty is that BAKER was the most impressive thing I have ever seen. A battleship thrown right into the sky like a toy! I took a certain amount of pride that our ship- Japanese though she might have been- was riding just fine at her anchorage. She was just deadly hot.

I was glad that I had dragged my full seabag along with me

this time. We would not be going back aboard or removing anything from her now. She was *hot*.

(ex-IJN Nagato after the BAKER blast. She is taking on some water, but we could not return to pump her out. Combat art by Art Beaumont. Image Navy historical and Heritage Command).

CLIMB MOUNT NIITAKA

His Imperial Japanese Majesty's Ship Nagato. Photo USN.

On 26 November, 1941, the Combined Fleet and its *Kidō Butai* (also known as the *Carrier Striking Task Force*) set sail from Hittokapu Bay in Japan's Kurile Islands under the overall command of Admiral Isoroku Yamamoto. He had personally selected the battleship *Nagato* as his flagship, the proud ship to lead the mightiest naval force ever to steam the Pacific Ocean.

Nagato had a bold look that Yamamoto appreciated, and she rode well as she sliced the waves at her best speed of twenty-six knots. She and her sister ship *Mutsu* had been built as *Dreadnaught*-class warships of 38,000 tons burden, 708 feet in length and nearly a hundred on the beam. Both had been extensively refitted with a unique seven-legged mast designed to maximize rigidity for range-finding purposes and survivability under shellfire.

The unique superstructure recalled the design of a pagoda, and consisted of a thick vertical leg in the center surrounded by six outer legs. The central leg was large enough to accommodate an electric elevator running between the foretop and main deck that carried the Admiral to his post on the flag bridge.

As peace talks continued in Washington, the ships made an undetected transit of the North Pacific to be in position for the contingency of war.

Peace was still a possibility. Yamamoto, a graduate of the US Naval War College and Harvard University, was confident that his bold plan to conduct a devastating surprise attack could secure an early advantage in a conflict against the United States. He was a realist, though, and knew that such advantage could not be guaranteed beyond the first year of war. He hoped for peace.

It did not come. Talks in Washington broke down. Admiral Yamamoto was directed to carry out his plan. On 2 December, the radio room in *Nagato* transmitted a message to the commander of the Kido Butai, Vice Admiral Chuichi Nagumo. The final decision had been made in Tokyo. It was to be war.

Yamamoto directed *Nagato's* radio room to send a message to the carrier striking force. The large vacuum tubes glowed orange with the power of the transmitter:

"NIITAKA-YAMA NOBORE 12 08" (新高山登れ12 08?). "Climb Mount Niitaka, 1208.

Admiral looked at the message from Yamamoto and looked at his chief of staff: "Hostilities will begin on December 7th, exactly as scheduled."

Admiral Isoroku Yamamoto. Photo USN

By the morning of December 7, from a position some 200 miles north of Oahu, six Japanese carriers began to launch the first attack wave. At 0753hrs, strike leader Commander Mitsuo Fuchida sent the signal "Tora! Tora! Tora!" indicating that the "lightning strike" on Pearl Harbor had achieved the element of surprise.

A staff officer raced the message from the *Nagato's* radio room to the Flag Bridge and handed the message to Admiral Yamamoto. The admiral nodded gravely. Now it was begun. It would be anyone's guess where and how it might end.

THE MANUSCRIPT

"The Nagato was the biggest battleship ever built. It could stand off and blow anything in the US Navy out of the water. We were scared witless of it, of its sudden appearance in the sea-lanes, and we searched unceasingly for it's whereabouts. The astonishing secret is in here - if you can read it." -JCR 11/16/1979

Those were the words my Uncle Jim typed on the cover sheet to the manuscript. He had it wrong, one of the few times I ever knew that to be true. He was thinking of the super battleship *Yamato*, which with her sister *Musashi* was one of two behemoths of the world ocean. *Yamato* was sunk as part of the assault on Okinawa, which our pal Admiral "Mac" Showers remembered well. We were talking about it at the Willow Bar a few years ago about the timing:

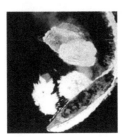

IJN Yamato under the final air attack that sank her. Photo USN.

"My roommate in the two-story Quonset hut on CINCPAC Hill was an army Captain named Hal Leathers. He did our ground estimates, and he thought there were 100,000 Jap troops waiting for us, and 2000 kamikaze aircraft ready to strike the Fleet.

"According to the traffic we decrypted, the biggest battleship in the world, IJN Yamato, was getting ready for a one-way mission to beach itself on the island and use its 18-inch guns as static artillery."

I marveled at the idea of taking one of the worlds greatest big ships to be used as static artillery while aground. "The Japanese were determined to make this so costly for us that we would seek options other than complete victory, right?"

"You have no idea. The civilians on Okinawa, like on Saipan, were indoctrinated to believe that the Americans would kill everyone on the island. Admiral Nimitz sent 1,500 ships, including some Brit fast carriers and a half million men."

1937 Photo With All Hands and Nagato's Pagoda Mast

Her operational history had some interesting moments. She carried supplies for the survivors of the Great Kanto Earthquake of 1923, and was dramatically upgraded in the mid-1930s to improve her armor and machinery. The iconic pagoda mast was added at that time. She was a participant in the Second Sino-Japanese War (1937) as the world slid into armed chaos, and had one of her two greatest moments on the 7th of December, 1941.

I pursed my lips. "Let me get the timing straight. The invasion started in April of 1945, didn't it?"

"April Fools Day," said Mac with a smile. "We found Yamato on the sixth, and sank her the next day. The Japs lost over 107,000 military and civilian on land and 4,000 sailors at sea.

It cost us almost seven thousand soldiers and another five thousand sailors to the kamikazes. It was something entirely new in battle, and it was a real problem. The running battle went on almost to the 4th of July..."

But Yamato was Mac's story, not Ed's. Uncle Jim had confused his battleships. He was actually talking about a ship called *Nagato*, which had a grand history and an amazing role to play even when the war was over. She was named for Nagato Province at the extreme western tip of the island of Honshu. She had been ordered while the Great War- the first of them- still raged in Europe. She was a *Dreadnaught*-class warship built as the lead ship in her class. She was not the biggest nor the newest battleship in the imperial fleet, far from it.

She still was an impressive 780 ft. LOA (Length Overall) and had a beam of 95 feet. Her armor belt was a foot of steel, and she carried four twin 41 cm guns as her main battery, with a wartime manning of over 1,700 officers and men.

Nagato was the flagship of Admiral Isoroku Yamamoto, and it was from her Flag Bridge that the order to attack the American Fleet was issued. As such, she is a special part of the history of her nation and ours.

Uncle Jim had been interested in her for something specialized: Jim was an engineer of the Old School, and fascinated by technology and how it developed in the 20th Century. A former Naval officer named Edward Smith Gilfillen had passed away in 1978, and his widow was interested in getting some of his lifetime of junk to people who would be interested in it.

Ed had been a member of the Naval Technical Collection team dispatched to Japan at the conclusion of the war. While at Yokosuka, he had the opportunity to board *Nagato* as she rode forlornly at anchor in Yokosuka Harbor.

IJN *Nagato* was moored at the entrance to Yokosuka harbor when the American Fleet arrived in the Sagami Wan. They were here to accept the unconditional surrender of the Empire. The Americans were wary, and startled by the appearance of the dreadnaught, but *Nagato* was there to witness, not fight. The Americans saw that her mighty guns were pointed fore - and - aft, not at battle stations. The big gray ships steamed slowly past- USS *South Dakota* (BB-57) was the first. Everyone was tense, not knowing what was going to happen to those arriving in the homeland of a fierce and implacable foe.

In order to prevent what Uncle Jim called "hanky-panky kamikaze games," Ed disassembled the ship's big radio, and had kept what Jim described as "18 huge radio tubes and a big variable condenser" as unique war souvenirs, given what they had transmitted on the very first Pearl Harbor day. As he was dying, he asked his wife to contact Jim to see that they were donated to the Antique Wireless Association's Museum in Bloomfield, NY, as unique specimens of WWII-era Japanese technology.

As far as I know, that is where they are to this day. But Ed

Gillfillen was going to get to know *Nagato* a lot better. In fact, he was going to be selected - or shanghaied - into being the XO on *Nagato's* last cruise.

That was the other thing that Jim got - the unpublished manuscript of Ed's account of the most remarkable experience a sailor can have.

Captain Sugino Shuichi arrived to assume command as last Japanese master of *Nagato*. Her previous Captain, RADM Otsuka Miki, had been killed at his post in the last American air raid in July of 1945. Shuichi was an officer of considerable combat experience and distinction, and now he was preside over the surrender of Japan's last operational ship-of-the-line.

That day of formal capitulation was only twelve days later, but before then, there was one thing Sugino could do to mitigate some of the sting of capitulation.

With surrender imminent, he had a sudden recollection of the fact that a lifeboat of the Czarist Russian battleship Orel was still displayed at Eta-jima Naval Academy, the Japanese bastion of tradition whose pride was as resolute as that of Annapolis. The lifeboat was a constant reminder to the Japanese midshipmen of the greatest moment of their Naval history: the victory of Admiral Togo over the forces of the Czar in the Tsushima Strait, the first time a Western colonial power had been vanquished by a rising Asian nation.

Now, it was the Japanese fleet doing the surrendering, and Sugino did not want to leave `trophies' for the Americans to exhibit in Annapolis. He sent word to gave orders to remove the imperial chrysanthemum crest from Nagato and had it burned on the afterdeck. It took nearly all of a day for the large crest to burn.

A golden seal similar to that worn by Nagato, this one adorning the bow of Admiral Togo's Mikasa, flagship at the battle of Tsushima Strait. Now again a memorial ship, in 1945 the Americans stripped the land-locked ship of its weapons and made it into a dance club during the Occupation.

That collision of pride and humiliation naturally led to misunderstandings. A pal wrote me yesterday with a sea story from the agonizing weeks of transition from martial independence to vanquished vassal.

Sid wrote: "Once upon a time in an O'Club in Okinawa, VQ-1 was flying VADM Frederic Bardshar, JR, the Commander of Task Force 77 from Vietnam to Atsugi, Japan, in an EA3B.

He was a great guy and a big man, probably 6'3 or 4". He was an aviator who flew and fought in WWII, becoming an air ace at the Battle of Leyte Gulf where he shot down eight Japanese aircraft in his F-6 Hellcat fighter."

F6F Hellcat preparing for deck launch. Photo USN.

"The EA3B pilot, navigator, and I went with him to one of the USAF Officer Club for dinner – in our flight suits. The USAF club managers didn't want to let us in, But VADM Bardshar noted that he saw USAF officers in the club in flight suits."

Club manager: "But they are on alert duty."

VADM Bradshar: "So are we, right out of Danang Air Base just a few hours ago."

"OK."

"While we were having dinner, he told us about that day aboard *Missouri*.

Immediately after the signing he was assigned to Shore Patrol in Yokosuka. He and his armed guards walked out the gates and never saw a live person on the streets. He reported that eerie fact to his seniors upon return to the base. He was told that it wasn't too surprising since the Japanese government had warned its people over the radio that they should stay indoors because the Americans would kill and eat their children."

"True story."

When I read it, I had to nod in agreement. The Occupation was a very strange thing, and some vestiges remained even in my time on the Sagami Wan decades later. I am surprised that the Occupation went as well as it did.

THREE FEATHERS AND A FLAG

RADM Donald "Mac" Showers is flanked by a pair of Socotras in the Hoyer Foyer at the Office of Naval Intelligence in Suitland, MD, on the occasion of Mac's donation of the battle flag of the IJN Battleship Nagato in 2012. The Foyer is so named irreverently in honor of the former House majority Leader Steny Hoyer, Maryland D-5th, for his efforts to have the new ONI building located in his district. Photo USN.

T he proud battleship *Nagato* had been pinned down in port for all of the last year of the war, and would not get underway again before the end. She was pier-side at the Yokosuka Naval Armory, heavily concealed with camouflage nets and plywood structures in July of 1945.

Soon-to-be Fleet Admiral William "Bull" Halsey had a personal thing about the ship from which the orders to attack Pearl Harbor had been issued, and he directed the THIRD Fleet to conduct a series of air raids on the base in order to put her underwater. Task Force 38, under Vice Admiral John S. McCain, was the blunt instrument of choice, and his force included nine fleet carriers, six light carriers, their escorts and a thousand aircraft.

On 10 July TF 38 pilots struck airfields around Tokyo and claimed to have destroyed 340 Japanese aircraft on the ground and two in the air. No Japanese aircraft responded to this attack as they were being held in reserve to mount large-scale suicide attacks on the Allied fleet during the impending invasion of the Home Islands. Mac Showers was unperturbed by the revisionist history about the use of the atomic bomb in later years. He and his pal Hal Leathers in the Estimates Section of the Forward Headquarters on Guam were reasonably confident that a million Americans would be killed or wounded in the assault, never mind the military and civilian population of Japan who stood in their path.

The strikes against Yokosuka were *Nagato's* last combat action, mostly serving as an American target.

Only two bombs actually hit the ship. One impacted the 01 deck aft of the mainmast, port side. It detonated at the base of the Number Three turret, and the occupying Americans of the Naval Technical Group marveled that although it had distorted the barbette, the turret was undamaged.

The blast scar left a nearly perfect image of the rising sun flag on the surface of the armor plate. Worse, it had penetrated the ceiling of the lightly armored deck near the wardroom, killing over twenty men.

There is some lingering controversy about a possible third hit. Something, possibly a five-inch rocket, tore through the port side stern and passed through the Admiral's mess and out the other side without exploding.

The technical team reported there was a gouge on the surface of the dining table, and markings that looked like they might have been made by teeth. The team was astonished that no one was killed there.

Between the two bombs, *Nagato* lost thirty-five officers and men.

The Allies lost fourteen planes and eighteen fliers, most of them over the harbor.

That was the last action of the war for the old battleship. Rear Admiral Ikeuchi Masamichi was recalled from retirement to assume command in late July due to the death of RADM Miki.

The newest Special Weapons of the Allies were employed against Hiroshima and Nagasaki on August 6th and 9th of August, respectively. At noon on the 15th, the Admiral called the crew to quarters to listen to the unprecedented broadcast of the Emperor, calling on his subjects to end hostilities.

On the 20th, Captain Sugino Shuichi, an active duty officer, arrived on the ship and there was a small change of command ceremony to make him the last Japanese commander. The position she occupied at the pier would be needed for other uses. Under his direction, Nagato was relocated to the Number One buoy in Yokosuka's inner harbor.

On the 28th, the Americans arrived. There are several accounts of who "captured" *Nagato*. The official legend is that "a boarding party composed of about 35 men from the USS *South Dakota*, took her symbolically on surrender day (Sep 2nd). The version some like to believe goes like this: "Many artifacts were brought back aboard USS *South Dakota*. The battle flag of the Nagato was acquired at this time."

Charles M. Cavell, QM1, USN, preserved a *Nagato* flag and donated it to the crew of USS South Dakota, and then the USS South Dakota Memorial in Sioux Falls, South Dakota.

Other credible reports of the disposition of the flag locker include this entry from the diary of the Skipper of the USS *Buchanan*, CDR Daniel E. Henry, USN, who reported this on August 30:

"Battleship *Nagato* boarded; San Diego docks at Yokosuka Naval Yard; first sighting of POWs; transferred 40 POW correspondents with horrifying reports on POW treatment. Awakened at 0700 and found the DD *Nicholas*

(DD-484,) captained by D.C. Lyndon, my first classmate at

the Naval Academy) was waiting to relieve us. They had met a Jap DD on the 27th and taken some Japanese prisoners to Admiral Halsey on the *Missouri*. We proceeded to anchorage but found our berth occupied by transports busy sending Marines ashore at Yokosuka. We anchored and watched the show. American planes are landing at the field at Yokosuka, says the commodore, but I am not sure.

At 0830, our APD (USS (Horace A. Bass (LPR-124) went alongside the BB *Nagato*, boarded, hauled down the Jap flag and hoisted ours. They report *Nagato* #10 boiler still warm, a diesel OK as is the anchor engine and steering gear. Other steam lines cut."

I think that may have been the first boarding right then. Others followed over the next few days.

We talked about the whole thing at the Willow Bar in Arlington where we gather to swap lies. There was more than one flag from the battleship, and our pal Mac got one of them. Now it is at ONI, and it hangs in a place of honor at the Office of Naval Intelligence out in suburban Maryland. ONI is a gleaming building of steel and glass, one of the last of the Cold War buildings to be erected to replace the crumbling old ones that had served in World War Two.

In the course of its construction, a former Director of Naval Intelligence had the high-security facility designated an official depository for the combat art commissioned by the Government. Accordingly, there are some spectacular original paintings dotting the corridors between the anonymous cipher-locked officers.

caught my boat for the seaplane tender from which I would depart the next morning for my return to Guam.

I didn't open the package until I was back in my private quarters on Guam, and then was pleased with what I had. I showed it only to Captain Eddie Layton, who confirmed I had a genuine souvenir."

"There's more that can be told, but that's the most authentic account of my procurement. In summary and in short, I'm sure there are other *Nagato* flags, but mine was clearly used, obviously had flown from the ship, and was from a believable source. More than that I cannot say." Mac raised his glass and took a sip.

"As I look back on the encounter and the bargain I struck, I now believe I could have talked the Marine out of all four of his flags in trade for the bottle of Three Feathers Whiskey I provided. But I was satisfied, I'm sure the Marine was, and I have no idea how he disposed of the other three flags."

Nagato was systematically plundered for the next few weeks, and formally stricken from the Navy List on the 15th of November 1945. Rust streaked the hull and the proud pagoda mast. The indomitable gulls of the Sagami Wan rendered their opinion of the works of man in streaks of white down the superstructure.

But that was not the last of the story, nor even the best part. That was going to come when the Last Battleship got a new crew. An American crew, and in the process, the enlisted ship-fitters discovered the *Nagato's* store of grain alcohol, which may not have been Three Feathers, but suited them just fine on the last deployment of the battlewagon.

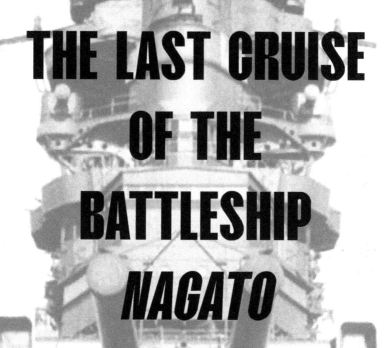

THE LAST CRUISE
OF THE
BATTLESHIP
NAGATO

Part One:

Meeting the XO

MEET THE XO

These Are the Words of Ed Gilfillen:

I t was one of those sleeps that are more than that: a retreat, a partial death, a cushioned slide into the past. From the cozy bunk of a Ship's cabin I had slipped back to the coast of Ceylon, living against in the wild beauty of the tropics. But there was something wrong: the nodding palms did not focus and on the horizon was a baleful yellow glow. With infinite labor, I climbed back into reality to see what had happened. It was a seaman squirting the light of a dim flashlight in my eyes. It seemed a long time before he spoke.

"Sir, there's salt water blowing on the starboard generator." His eyes popped a little. "It's coming right through the fan, Sir."

It took me a little time to adjust to this news. "Is the Chief down there?" I asked.

"Yessir."

I stretched in the luxurious manner of one who does not have to get up. My two cent's worth would be quoted at something less than that amid the mysteries of the engine room. With a bored "Very well," I turned over and went to sleep again, but that did not serve to get me back to Ceylon or anywhere else. I resented the next intervention by the flashlight.

"Sir," came the report. "It's all right now. The guy on the deck above had a leak in the bulkhead and he drained down a rat hole. He never looked to see where it went, but actually it went into an airshaft which filled up in time, as it would, naturally, and the water spilled over into the fan. It is all squared away now, we drained the duct."

All this was, of course, extremely interesting in the midst of a vague speculation as to where the water would appear next, so I drifted off into a dreamless sleep.

• • •

THAT NIGHT IS A fair sample of life in the *Nagato*. I was the XO to CAPT William J. Whipple, along with a handful of officers, chiefs and generally reluctant sailors. There were 180 of us all in total. We were an American crew trying to run a Japanese battleship. It was high adventure when we weren't too tired. We were to take the big ship to the Marshall Island for the CROSSROADS Atomic Bomb tests.

My first sight of *Nagato* came at the end of a seaplane ride to what I thought was Tokyo, but was actually south of Yokohama. The vast sprawl of the Kanto Plain made it difficult to ascertain what was what. At the terminal ship I was pushed with my gear into an open boat. Then began under a sullen sky a three-hour boat ride down into the lower Sagami Wan with sleet and spray stinging in over the bow of the utility boat. In spite of what I could do in the way of rigging tarpaulins, salt water worked its way through all my possessions.

Drenched and shivering, I had to shake saltwater .to make out the end of the breakwater ahead. The suggestion of shelter stimulated me to look around; there were ships at anchor in a harbor fringed by low brown hills. The scene was dominated by the sheer size of a red-rusted hulk with a pagoda-like superstructure forward. Below that loomed the black outlines of great guns, The Jack forward and the Stars and Stripes aft did not disguise the bulk of a Japanese Battleship. With a mental note to board her, sometime, I relapsed into the apathy of suffering.

When the *Nagato* was complete in 1920, she was without a doubt the most powerful warship of the time. Only the passenger ship *Leviathan* was larger. Her 41CM guns were a little bigger than any mounted in ships of the U.S. Navy, even to this day. With a turbo drive and high degree of electrification, she was in advance of her time. Through the twenties and thirties, she and her sister ship *Mutsu* were the core of the expanding Imperial Japanese Navy.

Even at the outbreak of the war, she was regarded as a first line ship, and the Japanese Commander-in-Chief Isoroku Yamamoto used her a flagship until just before the battle of Midway.

When hostilities began, she was in the Inland Sea. Sortieing several times in the early going, she was present at the battle of Midway, but did not sight any USN combatants. After that, she went with the rest of the IJN fleet to be based at the bastion atoll of Truk, and while in that operating area made calls in the Marshall Islands.

After the invasion of the Gilberts, she had to retire to Lingga Gulf near Singapore. As further invasions became imminent, she came out to Brunei Bay on the coast of Borneo to be ready to shield Palau, the Philippines, or the Marianas, whichever might be attacked.

In defense of Saipan, she came out through the San Bernardino Straits where she was attacked by a submarine but not hit. No other American forces were sighted, and she retired to Brunei Bay when the battle for he Marianas became hopeless.

When Leyte was invaded, she joined the task force that sortied through the San Bernardino Strait and got hit by two small bombs from a P-38 Lightning, which did some damage between her proud pagoda and stack. She sighted the Jeep Carriers of Task Group Taffy-3, and hit one of them with her main battery.

From there she returned to Japan and thence to Manila as a supply ship. From the P.I., she was dispatched to Yokosuka for a navy yard overhaul. By the time she arrived, a major decision had been made from Fleet Command: there would never again be enough fuel available in Japan to take her back to sea! The full significance of this was not to strike us until later.

Mounting a dozen twelve centimeter guns- the best anti-aircraft weapon the Japanese possessed- she was used in the defense of Tokyo Bay.

TABIS

My initial sight of the massive hill and pagoda of the ex-IJN *Nagato* came after arriving at Yokosuka by sea-plane. My next sight of her came as an incident of a scheduled air-voyage to Hokkaido.

We were weather bound a day in port, as nothing was flying to get us to the inspection sites up north. Fascinated by the big ship, I asked how I might get aboard for a tour. I was informed that visitors were not permitted on the *Nagato*, but after hooking a ride on a passing Mike boat, I found no resistance was actually offered at the gangway.

If I had known to look, I might have seen a signal flag run up from the flag bag on the pagoda to signal that an unknown officer was coming aboard, and any unscheduled non-regulation activities should be suspended immediately.

Nothing was quite what it seemed on the battleship, and I found that an unconducted tour of the ship was depressing, since it reflected the filth, destruction, confusion and all the drabness of war. The thrill of treading the deck of a Japanese Battleship lasted but a moment.

After a brief inspection, I was ready to go back ashore, and was intensely annoyed when I could not get a boat. As I paced off my bad humor on the forecastle, I was joined by a little Japanese fellow with a respectful manner.

He was wearing a pair of curious black leather, split-toed shoes called "tabis" on his feet. These were a type of unique outdoor footwear worn by construction workers, farmers, painters, road workers, rickshaw-pullers and others since the late Meiji Period in Japan.

The most distinctive characteristic of Tabi Shoes is the split-toe design that separates the big toe from the other toes. This feature enhances their comfort and stability, important qualities in a shipboard environment. The sole of traditional Tabi shoes are made of pliable natural rubber which is soft enough to be flexible, but stiff enough to protect the wearer's foot from ground debris.

The little fellow wore a frayed mustard-colored uniform with a matching cap with a short brim, almost like Japanese military fatigues. His face was nearly toothless and his skin was as gray as a mouse.

In a mixture of Spanish, Portuguese and Italian he related who he was. He gestured as he said his name was Matano, and that he was an electrical engineer who had graduated from the University of Sao Paulo, and had practiced his profession twenty years in Brazil. Returning to Japan for a visit in the fall of 1941, he had been caught in the toils of the war.

Strange phenomena and tales of harrowing adventure were no longer a novelty to me; I listened to his tales of bomb-dodging not out of interest but from sheer boredom as I scanned the harbor for a boat to hail and return ashore. If I had thought about him at all, it was to tick him off subconsciously as one of the resident ghosts of the massive haunted warship. But I was to think much of him, and his formidable skills, later on in a desperate dark night far from shore.

And to be intensely thankful I had made his acquaintance that foul day at the anchorage in the Sagami-wan. At that point, I had no idea I was to be the Executive Officer of this ghost ship, or custodian of the well-being of the merry pirates who would take her on her last voyage.

GENERAL QUARTERING

Nagato's appearance had been altered from her war-time look when I first saw her. There was plywood and camouflage stacked all over the superstructure to distract the American pilots. To render her less conspicuous, the tops of her mainmast and stack had been cut off and plywood structures erected on her decks. Rust blended in with the forlorn hills ringing the Yokosuka Ko, but a few patches of brown, green and black paint were added. No doubt she was difficult to see, but the July raiders of 1945 found her and scored two major hits.

Just before hostilities eased, her crew left her, abandoning ship, so to speak. They may have looted her as well, though much food was left aboard. After that, she was systematically exploited by various American units who took even her electric-blue plush upholstery and smashed what they could not carry away.

Seen from a distance, *Nagato* had a low, rakish and characteristically Japanese profile which gave her something of the appearance of a submarine. The resemblance was not wholly by chance; the designers had put most of the bulk of the ship below the waterline where it could not be hit by naval gunfire. It was also reflected in her trimming gear. Instead of flooding tanks on the opposite side to trim, as a surface ship normally does, she blew her tanks on the same side like a U-boat. This has the disadvantage of requiring dangerous high-pressure airlines but it cancels loss of buoyancy due to a hit instead of doubling it.

Her freeboard was less than that of any American ship of comparable size. Later, we were to put her lee rail underwater like a racing yacht. Hers was a fierce, grim outline - not a nice thing to see looming through the mist.

Her main decks were wood laid on steel. The space forward of the number one turret was devoted to anchor gear as in our naval ships. The system was so simple that one man could perform the sea and anchor duty without assistance, if need be. The system was so rugged that it could go without maintenance for long periods. From two holes in the deck, the chains came up around power capstans that gripped them, routing them straight forward to great steel nostrils in the bow.

Puttering about the forecastles in the gray light of early morning, I used to marvel at these chains, for every link weighed more than a hundred pounds. This fact was to be brought forcefully to my attention several times during the last cruise of the last capital ship of the Imperial Navy.

Standing in the eyes of the ship with your back braced against the wind, you could appreciate the sweep of the deck back to the muzzles of the guns with the squat turrets behind them.

From there, you might glance up to the slotted steel box from which the Admiral and the Captain used to watch the course of battle. Behind that towered the pagoda, mighty in its complexity of detail: battlements, , catwalks, bridges, guns, range-finders, revolving anti-aircraft turrets, radar search-lights, signal-yards and platform upon platform piled up for 150 feet. Inside the pagoda was a mass of switchboards, offices and living spaces, every compartment with an oxygen bottle for protection against gas attack.

There even was an elevator to take the Admiral as high up as he wanted to go.

The heart of this edifice was the conning tower already mentioned, a steel box with slotted walls a foot thick. One entered through a bank-vault style hatch. The narrow windows had been cleverly placed to give an unobstructed view three-quarters of the way around the compass. Inside were a steering wheel and gyrocompass repeater, the engine room telegraph and dials to show the speed of the ship, what the engines and rudders were doing and where the guns were pointed.

On the port side- the place of honor in Japan- was the Admiral's upholstered settee. Few Americans could stand upright in the conning tower, but otherwise it was roomy. From the back wall was a cluster of speaking rubes and telephones that led to all communications centers in the ship. The tower had taken a direct hit from a heavy bomb without any of the instruments being damaged. In the heat of battle, the occupants may not have even noticed the explosion.

Most of the arrangements about the ship were conventional, reflecting British practice more than the American style. Baths were special- there wasn't a single shower in the ship. Instead, there were burnished copper tubs so deep you could sit in them on a little wooden stool and just peep over the edge. In this fashion the Japanese sailor takes his scalding bath. In Officer country the tubs were single.

American sailors use the Japanese bath on Nagato. Photo USN.

The crew had bigger ones, ten or more bathing at a time. Sanitary arrangements were of all sorts, from high stools one had to climb up on through scuttles to the old-fashioned *benjo* toilets.

Room furniture was like that of a passenger liner of the 1920s, including polished metal wash-bowls that folded away out of sight when not in use and which drew water from a tank that had to be filled by a steward. There was no piping of any sort. Interior decoration was along somber British lines; oak panel effects were so cleverly painted on molded sheet steel that you had to tap to be sure what was real wood and what was not.

Wood and metal were, in fact, mingled throughout the design, with the more easily fabricated material being used for each part, Drawers were mostly wood, panels were mostly constructed of metal. Bunks were arranged just the same way as in our ships.

Officers were served Japanese-style breakfasts- but European lunches and dinners. The men had rice with pickled rashes, canned fish, soy sauce and occasional delicacies such as salmon, crabmeat or pickled tangerines. Apparently they ate where they worked and lived, squatting on mats behind gun shields or in the passageways. Food was fetched from the galley by one of the sailors in the duty section.

This system has many advantages. No one who has witnessed the chaos and confusion on US Navy ships when General Quarters is sounded at night will deny the strengths of this system. On our ships men come running half the length of the ship to their GQ stations. We used to say it this way: "All hands forward run aft, all hands aft run forward and all hands amidships block passageways."

The Japs didn't miss a chance for education: in their leisure time, the sailors studied silhouettes of American aircraft painted on bulkheads and gun-shield everywhere throughout the ship.

The officers lived in the extreme after-part of the ship on two decks: senior above and juniors below. Originally, these had larger port-holes than any of our ships. These compartments very comfortable or even luxurious; truly pleasant places to live.

The Admiral's Mess was a large room extending right athwart the stern and had skylights and electric fans for ventilation. Aft of this was what we called a 'shrine room,' also with a skylight and fans where pictures of the Emperor, Empress and Crown Prince were kept.

There was also a desk in this room, which was used only by the Commander-in Chief of the Japanese Fleet, and thus must have been used by Admiral Yamamoto himself.

With the coming of war, the ports were sealed off, spoiling the whole effect. We used the Admiral's mess as a wardroom, since *Nagato*'s original wardroom was completely destroyed by a bomb hit in July. But we wouldn't have used it anyway, since it was a dingy, noisy place, cold in winter and hot in the tropics. All the officers would have gladly traded their traditional quarters for rooms up forward that still had their portholes for ventilation, but our sailors had got on board first, and it was wisely decided by Captain Whipple not to try to evict them.

The cruise south was going to be hard enough as it was. We didn't need to add resentment to the challenge of learning how to operate a ship with all the instructions written in Japanese!

NAVAL ARCHITECTURE

Two members of the Nagato's IJN crew in 1942. Photo IJN archives vis USN.

I have to state that life on *Nagato* was as much a cultural experience as an engineering one. There was something new to discover each day, and sometimes each hour as new challenges presented themselves.

We are all products of our own cultures. The design of USN ships, for example, are shot through with definite principles, all born of experience and most have the force of an article of faith. We American sailors like clean lines. No matter how useful a ladder, a pad eye, an anchor platform or bearing for an outboard davit might be, we cannot have them. We hoard space and weight with single-minded intensity. If a pump can be made a little smaller or lighter by using alloy steel bearings and supplying the highest-grade lubricating oil under pressure, we do it.

Around the guns we allow exactly enough space to protect the men from the recoil - not an inch more. Cleanliness aboard our ships matches that of hospitals. If that requires a clean sweep-down six times a day and a quarter of the crew busy chipping pain, no matter. By which is called "preventative maintenance," we keep our ships always in fighting condition. It is a way of thought which has produced the most effective ships in existence, and which won the war in the Pacific.

Japanese practice is different, or at least it was before the Imperial fleet was reduced to *Nagato* alone. This ship was roomy, to a degree, even in the turrets. Machinery was simple, rugged and large, made of easily-obtainable materials with plenty of room around it to maneuver. There was no such thing as preventive maintenance. Engines were designed to operate a long time without repair and then to be replaced in a Navy shipyard. The crew was there to fight, not to clean ship; every aspect of their lives focused on the single issue of battle. This is in marked contrast to our way of doing business, which was to keep the ship squared away and ready for action.

Other navies of the world operate closer to the Japanese principles than to those of the US Navy. The war has just proved that our way is superior. Whether it will continue to be best in the face of new developments seems problematical.

During the July air raids of 1945, *Nagato* was hit on the port anchor chain, losing the anchor and holing the bow just above the water line. The patch placed over this rent in the hull was going to give us trouble later. Another large bomb entered the superstructure just under the catapult deck, exploding on the face of the Number 5 barbette, on which it etched a mark that resembled a rising sun, The face of the steel was left smooth at the point of impact. From there out the metal was spattered and gouged in outward as though a firecracker has exploded on softened butter. The interior of the barbette was quite un-injured - the face of the turret was protected by nearly a foot of armor steel.

The space around the barbette had been cluttered with ventilating shafts, bulkheads, and other impediments, but all of these were carried away by the blast that also bulged the deck over it upward. The result was to form a large hall, partially open to the weather where we later showed the movies. At sea, waves sometimes burst in through the shattered bulkhead, swishing and gurgling through the chair legs as the movie-goers raised their feet out of the water without taking their eyes off the action on the screen.

Some sort of projectile traveling upward entered the wardroom to port and went out to starboard without detonating. I don't know whether anyone was in the compartment at the time, but there were marks on the table that might have been made by teeth. I have no idea what it might have been.

The gross detail of the engineering equipment and spaces of *Nagato* were obvious enough, and conventional in appearance, but the piping and trunk system was so complex that we were never able to use it with any certainty. All about the deck, and below, were hand wheels to open and close valves. The problem for us was that in most cases, the valve was not co-located with the wheel. The turning force from the wheel was transmitted through Rube Goldberg-style reach rods to the actual valve. These in turn were routed right through bulkheads and inaccessible spaces. To have traced them all would have been a prohibitive effort and we did not bother.

Some were important, though, and we had to investigate by direct observation, sometimes helped by Japanese inscriptions, sometimes by experiment to see what happened when we turned them. We managed to identify some of the more important valves, but there was always an element of doubt.

One night in Yokosuka, the petty officer of the watch noticed that the end of the accommodation ladder had sunk underwater. He took a sailor's fatalistic view of that and joisted it out, but when it went under again he thought it worthwhile to call the Command Duty Officer. Investigation revealed what had occurred. A visitor to the quarterdeck had turned a hand-wheel on deck out of idle curiosity and had managed to flood the Number 3 Magazine!

We scrambled around and had to bring a tug alongside the mooring to pump it out again. I always had the feeling that some of the crew knew far more about the valves than the officers did.

In fact, several times I seemed to hear a disgruntled sailor mutter: "I know just where that valve is!"

They could have sunk the ship at any time without risk of being identified and court-marshaled. All I knew was that sailors are sailors the world over, and many of our guys thought the war was over and wanted to go home, not steam a Japanese battle-wagon to the Marshall Islands to blow it up with an atom bomb.

WATER, WATER EVERYWHERE

The situation with respect to water and oil tanks was a nightmare. Most of the valves controlling the fluids were inaccessible and one could never be sure they were completely closed. There was no reliable way to find out what or how much was in the tank.

Oil circulated through the ship continuously; it might be anywhere. From the same tank one might get night got oil one day, nothing the next, the salt water and perhaps after a week oil again. We kept watch over the side and knew that all the oil we took stayed with us until it went up the stack.

We did not know how much was in the ship to start with, nor could we be sure how much of the tanker pumped in was actually salt water. Some of the most conventionally-minded officers had difficulty adjusting to the situation.

The idea of shortages of fresh water brings sailing vessels and oak casks to mind, but we had the same problem with a modern twist in the *Nagato*. We were distilling five or six tons an hour from seawater. Much of that went into the boilers. Theoretically, they use the same water over and over again, but some was lost each pass through the mass of not-so-tight steam pipes. What did come back was always contaminated with seawater. This would make the boilers sick and they would vomit to the sky as the steam roiled and have to be purged into the bilges.

We would have liked to use water drained from the boilers in the laundry, but never found a practical way to get it there. What would be spared from the boilers was pumped into the fresh water arteries of the ship and some of it actually got to faucets, but most of it mixed with saltwater seepage in remote compartments.

We were always looking for those locks, forming the habit of tasting anything that dripped, and we finally stopped many of the leaks, but our fresh water accounts never came anywhere near balancing.

What with all this food scattered about - the Japanese crew ate at their duty stations, unlike the USN which had dedicated mess decks and wardrooms, it was inevitable that there should be rats in the ship. We were told by Commander Inoda, *Nagato's* former First Lieutenant, that during the Japanese reign "there were always very many (rats)."

Actually, the rats were not much bother and never a cause of sickness, as far as I could tell. I valued them as indicators of the ship's seaworthiness. I figured that if they ever started to make the gangway *en mass*, I would have been right there with them along with my seabag. The only protest came when some officers tried to sleep on deck in the base of Number Four Turret. The rats came out in force, chasing each other around the turret, hissing and squeaking. After hearing about such things for a long time, we were at last caught in a rat-race.

ALL BETS ARE OFF

IJN Sakawa, fitting out at Sasebo Naval Base in 1945. She never fought, but served to bring home some of the 3.5 million Japanese troops stranded overseas at the end of hostilities in a great arc from Manchuria to the Solomons, and across the islands of the Central and Southwest Pacific. Photo USN from IJN archives.

I had originally been sent to Occupied Japan as part of the technical collection team tasked with examining the war machine we had just defeated. It was a big job, and there were places to visit all over the Home Islands.

Not long after returning from the snow-buried villages of Hokkaido on an inspection tour to collect and assess items of Japanese war technology, I was ordered to the *Sakawa*, the only remaining Japanese cruiser. She was an *Agano*-class cruiser, second built. Named after a river in Kanagawa Prefecture, she would wind up with us at Bikini. *Sakawa* had been intended for use as a flagship for a destroyer flotilla, but never saw combat duty, since she was completed at the yard in Sasebo in 1945. She had a graceful and uncluttered deck line with a single stack and had suffered no war damage, so she was a rare pristine example of the Japanese shipbuilding art, at least from a distance.

At the time of her surrender, her guns were removed; later she had made two trips to Wekwak and one to the Palava returning Japanese prisoners to the homeland. When I boarded her with a group of American officers, the Japanese flag was still flying from her masthead, which may have made her the last actual IJN ship afloat. It was a bitter winter day. Sleet and sheets of spray were driven over the bow of the boat. It was painful to look ahead. *Sakawa's* decks were deserted. We waited a moment, looking for the Officer of the Deck, but seeing no one, we entered the superstructure.

At the top of a ladder, we found a little blue-uniformed Japanese boy who stared at the group of us uniformed Gaijins for a moment and then ducked below. Presently, a middle-aged Japanese in a formal blue uniform with chrysanthemums in his collar appeared and motioned us to descend. He was the Captain. We entered his cabin, an elegantly furnished compartment complete with portholes, a fine mahogany table, upholstered settee and an ornate desk of the type so often seen in the Orient.

Whiskey was served all around as the Captain introduced his senior officers. Then we made a tour of the ship. The decks, navigation spaces, and radio rooms were in perfect order with al fittings and instruments visible and working. Engineering equipment and spaces were modern and well kept up. There was some poor welding in evidence, but that was to be expected in a vessel finished so late in the war.

The living spaces, however, were neither clean or in order. In most of them an extra wooden deck had been inserted, doubling the sleeping space but leaving little head room. The whole ship smelled of human bodies and stale food. On the fantail were wooden troughs for washing and wooden privies that hung out over the water. Such were the necessities of the reparation services. In spite of the smell and improvised nature of the accommodations, there could be no doubt that the Sakawa was a going concern.

I became quite well acquainted with these officers and others, including a rear admiral who helped us on the *Nagato*. No amount of prejudice could disguise the fact that they were capable professionals would do well in any navy in the world.

At the high levels of the Occupation there were policy debates about what should be done with the captured materiel of the war machine. Clearly, these relics of the Greater East Asia Co-prosperity Sphere would have to go- and perhaps a test of the new Atom Bomb might be the best use for them.

As the largest remaining capital ship, and the symbol of the attack on Pearl, it was decided that *Nagato* should be manned by a brave band of American volunteers and adventurers who could accommodate the unexpected and unusual with aplomb, and none-the-less be completely Navy in terms of the ortho-doxy of their views, and more than capable of sustaining any difficulty which might be in the offing.

The officers would lead harassed subordinates who cherished the "points" they had accumulated to prioritize their eligibility for demobilization and a trip back to the land of the Big PX.

The sailors were uniformly tired of the War, the Navy and Japan, in that general order, and their main object was to get home without a nervous breakdown. The problem of building a crew for the last battleship was a challenge. They had to get a list of 180 names from a naval establishment desperately short on men. They would do it in such a way as to minimize contact with angry individuals.

By one of those bits of luck (without which nothing works in this man's Navy), we got a handful of petty officers just in from de-commissioned vessels. About a third of the rest came straight from Boot Camp, while the remaining sailors were Shanghaied by levy imposed on the commanding officers of ships currently in the harbor.

It would have been more than human for officers in that position not to send their boat-adjusted men and these skippers were very human. Many whose points would come due in a few months were included. Not one man aboard was a volunteer.

This was an era of corrosive cynicism on the waterfront in Yokosuka. Everyone as concentrating on getting home, and when frustrated on that front, the endless quest to find their *own* souvenirs. Any old excuse for disobedience of orders would be accepted by officers, who feared that any official motion they might take might delay their own release to deal with holding mast or bringing a court-marshal.

View from Nagato's damaged Pagoda of USS South Dakota. Watercolor on Scratch Board by Standish Backus; 1945. Image Naval History and Heritage Command.

It was from this atmosphere that men came to the *Nagato*, a ship stripped by scavengers and herself being the biggest souvenir ever lifted. It is not surprising that all of us considered that all bets were off. Sailors and officers proceeded to adjust themselves pragmatically to conditions as they found them.

Their first impression of the *Nagato* was not reassuring. Everything but the hull seemed damaged beyond repair. In fact, it was hard not to believe the scuttlebutt that the battle-ship would never steam again under her own power, and that all this was just another foul-up, and that what they did really did not matter. Before the arrival of responsible officers, they sensed a lack of leadership and lack of plan, and were morally damaged thereby.

Enterprise and ability to adjust to circumstances are American characteristics. These men did not long waste time being sorry for themselves. They found a diesel-electric plant on board. It was intended for emergency use, but they started and ran it until it wore out. Meanwhile they had lights and electric heaters in every room, hotplates on which to cook chow, and so were able to live in comfort. By the time the emergency diesel was burned out, they had a boiler operating on salt water and one of the steam driven electric generators working. The salt water ruined the boiler, but before it was completely gone, they had distilled enough to start another boiler on fresh water, and after that they could make enough fresh water for washing and cooking.

They selected the best staterooms in the ship – those having portholes – scrubbed and painted the walls, arranged places of honor for their precious pin-ups, ransacked the rest of the ship for furniture and found that the rapacious souvenir hunters had overlooked much good stuff including Japanese food.

Soon they were living better than anyone afloat in the bay. They reconstructed the radios left on board and got them working for entertainment and a loose command and control. They rearranged the ship's public address system to pipe music everywhere. All the while, they were exploring the more remote fastness of the ship. The ship-fitters discovered a store of grain alcohol, had it analyzed, found it drinkable. Later I tried hard to find it, but never did. There are some secrets Sailors know to keep to themselves.

There was no need to bother with the formalities of the Plan of the Day, like reveille, Quarters for muster, or liberty lists. Instead, they got up when it felt right, ate and went ashore as they pleased. It was a sailor's dream, clouded only by the thoughts that someday someone might want them to do something.

Let him who rails against the ancient officer's caste-system first live in an unsupervised detachment of enlisted men. He will find out how hard class distinction can really be driven. The crew broke up into little groups of professional people intensely jealous of their prerogatives. The signalmen took over the pagoda and industriously got the Japanese signal lights going. They rigged a flag-bag and signal pennants, and thus got in touch with other similar groups of signalmen all over the harbor.

Once established in the larger brotherhood of those who know what is going on, they were able to warn of impending visits by dignitaries and of the birth of policy.

The ship-fitters were a hunter clan – the only ones who knew exactly where all the desirable stores were, and ready to tell the right people for a consideration in kind. Under the spur of private enterprise, they became more thoroughly familiar with the ship than any regular regime could have made them. That intimate knowledge of detailed arrangements was later to save her from sinking.

Under the stimulus of professional rather than material mo-
tives, the electricians likewise put forth a mighty effort during
those free-and-easy days. They had a sound appreciation of
the principles of electricity, but little practical experience. On
a proper man-o-war they would have been rewarded for good
conduct by being allowed to knock off paint-chipping once in
a while to screw in electric light bulbs. In *Nagato* they could do
anything that struck their fancy, and they did.

All conceivable material was there at hand: big generators,
wire of all sizes, motors, vacuum tubes, batteries, communication circuits. They could work with thousand amperes or a
thousandth of an ampere, as they pleased. Their services were
in demand; they could ask and get anything they wanted for
rigging hot plates, radios, special telephones, etc. When something went wrong and burned up, as so often happened to the
electrical equipment, it was only to be expected in view of the

rundown condition of the ship. If a motor went "phut," they knew just where there was another like it.

Giving their imaginations full reign, they produced some weird Rube Goldberg contraptions to make life easier. Experience gained during this period of experimentation paid off later when the electrical system became a menace to the survival of the ship. No one could tell them what to do then, and no one had to. You would see them plodding wearily along the dripping corridors, tired, grey-faced, streaked with dirt, but carrying on whole days without sleep, doing all that would be done.

The ship had had an elaborate communication system; there were several control switchboards and phones hanging on almost every bulkhead in battle clamps from which they could not be dislodged by the shock of gunfire. Whether the electricians ever understood this system completely I did not know, but probably *they* did.

They never put the switchboards into full operation but, grudgingly it seemed, they connected permanently the few lines needed to operate the ship. Phones so activated officially were tagged Most of the untagged phones hanging on the bulk heads were dead, but not all; each clan of enlisted men had its own private system known only to its members. Those were used mostly to prevent narrow-minded individuals from seeing anything that might disturb them.

Such was the situation facing Captain Whipple when he took over. Neither the ship nor the crew were ready for sea. The one had to be got in condition mechanically and the other brought to the state of discipline without which any ship is but a floating coffin.

Discipline must be tough with bread in one hand and a stick in the other: privileges to grant and punishment to inflict. Neither was easy. You cannot offer thrills to a man who believes that the great and final adventure of his life will be his return home. You could not offer privileges ashore. The town of Yokosuka and the Honcho-ku ginza outside the gate was so depressing that most men preferred to remain onboard.

The usual Navy punishment for minor offenses is extra duty, but the smallness of this crew and the bulk of the ship made it necessary to demand extra work of everyone. To have used confinement as a punishment would have required setting a guard on this brig – there were just not enough men to do it. The final resort of a bad-conduct discharge would not only lose a irreplaceable man, but is scarcely applicable to youngsters – it is wrong to mark a man for life for a minor indiscretion of youth.

Captain Whipple's status was further complicated by the

anomalous status of the ship. Though not a ship of the US Navy, it was flying the Jack forward; aft, she flew the Stars & Stripes without being recognized under them. She had been officially declared not a prize of war, but no one had said just what she was. She was a study in ambiguity. Captain Whipple had been designated commanding officer, but not by the President, whose prerogative that is.

Courageously laying himself open to actions in the civil courts, he decided to assume the disciplinary duties of a regular commanding officer. My own theory was that since the ship was not registered under any flag, she was subject only to the unwritten law of the sea – that her officers were not bound by the troublesome restrictions of Navy Regulations or union contracts, and in fact – but never mind that now. The officers soon found that these men could not be driven. One could call for a working party and get it; but the minute his back was turned, the men would melt away into the caverns of the ship where no one could find them.

An officer would explain how he wanted a thing done and go to the wardroom for a cup of coffee, but nothing would come of it; he could inquire why and be told that the necessary materials could not be found. Being sure that the men know full well where the materials were was no help – he didn't. Any attempt to stand by and instruct the men step by step was frustrated by passive resistance; they would stand, helpless, asking, "What do I do know, Sir?" as though they had never seen anything done like that before.

In time, even the dumbest officers realized that the men could not be driven, and one or two of them found that they could actually be *led*.

MONTANO

So, as the mighty battleship rides at anchor outside the break-water in the Sagami-wan, it is time to talk about how important the little man I first met in my impromptu tour of the battleship. I considered him an apparition of the ship, which clearly was haunted by the history of what she had done as part of the attack on Pearl Harbor.

The cultural side of the international cooperation was furnished by him, Matano, the electrical engineer and one of the resident ghosts of *Nagato*. Matano-san somehow emerged as the vital middle-man between the Americans and the Japanese workers who were brought aboard each day to help prepare us for the long voyage to the Marianas for the demonstration of the power of the atom. He was a muscular little man of about forty, with bulging spectacles. He wore an armband signifying rank, but was otherwise dressed like the others in mustard fatigues and black split-toed shoes that made me think of the feet of frogs. There was nothing perfunctory about the services rendered; he loved work, accomplishment and discipline for their own sake. With us on *Nagato*, he was just as happy with us as he had ever been under the Emperor.

I would judge that he probably found one naval officer quite like another, regardless of national origin: all of us unreasonable and inconsistent, and all completely comfortable in imposing impossible tasks on him and his workers. That notwithstanding, we developed a mutual liking and understanding which smoothed over many difficulties between our cultures, and I am sure he was as sorry when we sailed south as I was to lose his services.

To the men he was simply known as "Montana," and he was as integral a part of the ship as the great guns. He had the run of the place, and was occasionally useful as an interpreter. In view of the strict rule that no American food could be given to the Japanese, it was astonishing how the old man fattened on air.

A carefully lettered sign "Y. Matano, Office and Quarters"

had appeared over one of the hatches when I paid a visit down there one day.

He had a desk, a cot and blankets in a spot close enough to the boilers to be cozy. Much of his time was spent lettering signs in English or Japanese, as requested, and much of the rest inscribing "memorials" to me, of which the following are samples:

NECESSITY OF SHIP'S BOAT

On Sunday, Monday, Tuesday & Wednesday (today), I saw at the Officer's Landing (from where those Jap workmen come up in the morning) the following:

Boat situation *is getting day by day harder, and, if the ship wants to have them on board at fixed time, punctually, in every morning, then the ship should have her own BOAT to them at the Officer's Landing, sending every morning their big size Boat, while she wants them before her leave. If the Ship relies on the efforts of the Yard Crafts Office, the Ship will not have them at the fixed time every morning. They are waiting for Boat, from 7:30 every morning, at the said Landing point, wasting 2-3 hours without working.*

The necessity of checking-up with regards to the GUARD who take charge in these jap workmen. For an example, this morning he came down to the GATE to take them in, just at about 9:00. He used to appear at the GATE at 7:50 to 8:00, formerly. The action of their GUARD, from the GATE to the Landing (where he gets boat for them) and the carrier-BOAT are 2 important factors.

JAP WORKMEN STOLEN

According to the Jap foreman, some of those Jap workmen have been stolen from their money and watch, on board the Ship. And it is likely to be "<u>many cases</u>." This is causing a kind of consternation in their morality.

If it be so, I hope that the Ship's side takes it into consideration, <u>MODERATELY</u>. A satisfactory result will not come from an abrupt measure.

To the men, having Matano around seemed perfectly natural. They treated him with the same affectionate fondness formerly bestowed on an old, dependent Uncle George in their own homes.

To the Japanese foreman, there was nothing mysterious about either officers or crew; they were just like all the other naval people he had known. But to Matano, a man of the world, the whole *Nagato* episode was a seething turmoil of contradictions. Loving this ship, he was glad to see her active again, but distressed that an enemy should tend her holy decks.

He was a devotee of rules and adherence there to, but glad to see rules broken in his favor. He was loyal to his fellow Japanese, but in minor disagreement he was continually finding that the Americans were right. He found himself coming to like Americans whom he ought to hate.

What really burned him up, though, was that the American government should pay his daughter more than it paid him. He couldn't understand why.

I did not tell him that to the young men of the American Fleet so far from home, there was something his daughter could offer them that he *never* could.

LIBERTY PARTY

Though I slept through few nights outside the breakwater, what with one thing or another carrying away, I remember particularly the visit of the liberty party from the *General Butner* (AP-113).

There was no need for anyone to wake me. Heavy blows against the hull, shouting, the pounding of running feet on deck, were conclusive that something had come adrift. I slipped on a pair of overshoes and one of those fine hooded great-coats the Army issues for foul weather, and vaulted up the ladder into the thirty-knot gale tinged with puffs of whirling snow.

Running over to the port side, where the noise was, I peered down. A tank lighter was tied up there. I was checked her lines-before turning in, but then she was empty. Now I looked down on a lot of people. As my eyes accommodated to the dark, I made out officers in blues without overcoats, soldiers, sailors in dress blues without pea-coats and a Negro steward.

The immediate problem was not how they got there, but how to get them aboard before they froze. The tank lighter was bucking and plunging against the side of the ship; it seemed impossible to get them out without crushing someone in between. We lowered a cargo net, but their hands were too numb to grasp it, and some were too terrified to try, but we got a few that way.

Then someone noticed that every fourth or fifth wave reared up the ladder-like ramp of the lighter to the level of our deck. We made them climb it one by one, as a crew of six deck hands picked them off on the rise, like ripe fruit. Our galley had been manned; as each came aboard, he was hurried down there for a cup of hot coffee while the Master-at-Arms broke out cots in the warm compartment near the boilers. No one was hurt.

Then we got the story. They were the liberty party of the *General Butner*, a transport that had shipped out of San Francisco in January of 1946, with ports of call at Yokohama, Shanghai and Tsingtao supporting our efforts to save the Nationalists in China. Somehow the Liberty Party had missed the last boat back to the ship.

There had been no place for them to sleep at the landing, and the addled Beachmaster had loaded them all into a small landing craft, dreaming no doubt, that it was the Ark. As soon as they turned the breakwater, it began to fill with seawater. The crew had very little time. They saw our great bulk and made for it, dumping the passengers into the tank lighter and running for the beach. Later we heard they made it.

The only noteworthy sequel came next morning.

One of our officers, who had a big night on the beach, felt his way up the passage to the wardroom and peered in. He seemed to see Marines, rubbed his eyes, but could still see them. He tottered back to his room for his glasses, came back but, it was no go, they were still there. He sat down and ate his cornflakes glumly, without a word, passing the whole thing off as one of the mysteries of the *Nagato.*

SHACKLES

rowsing around the Navy Yard in Yokosuka looking for likely opportunities, one of our officers found an anchor stamped with the name *"Nagato."* It was a huge thing, as befits a hook intended for a dreadnaught and nothing would do but we must have it onboard to replace the one lost in the chaos of the last American bombing of the harbor.

Never mind that it weighed twenty tons.

The operation was carefully planned. Personnel at the Yard

were assigned to pick the anchor up and put it on the deck of the large tank lighter. A floating crane was to accompany the lighter to our side, draw out the end of our anchor chain and lower it to the deck of the tank lighter where we would be ready to shackle it on the anchor. Then, as we heaved in on the chain, the crane was to pick up the anchor, and when we had all but a few links hove in, they were supposed to let the anchor down until it hung from the chain and go their way in peace.

It didn't work like that. The anchor was in the tank lighter, all right, but the Jap-operated crane hooked onto it and hoisted it out without bothering with our chain. They hoisted it right up over our deck where it slipped and flopped about as the crane teetered on the swells, lending its full weight to the ensuing negotiations. The deck began to fill with jabbering Nipponese, some coming up over the side and others inexplicably from the rear.

I was standing fast, insisting that they put it back in the lighter and start all over again, but I noticed the whites of the boatswain's mate's eyes as they flashed between the crowd, the mighty anchor and its pendulous arc.

Although the day was cold, beads of sweat glistened on the Boatswain's forehead. So, I let them lower it on deck, which they accomplished with scarcely a bump. Then, having delivered the anchor, they were all for getting back to their warm quarters. If I had let them, the anchor would have stayed right there for as long as the battleship lasted.

We are at the mooring outside the breakwater, and except

for the floating crane there was no way to move it. So, I made them haul a hundred feet of chain out through our bow chocks while our crew let down the safety lines on that part of the deck.

Chock from an IJN Battleship on display at the Kure Naval Museum. Photo Punynari

The Japs brought the chain back on board and put it down by the anchor, leaving a bight of chain hanging over the side. The boatswain was ready to shackle it onto the anchor but the shackle weighed four hundred pounds and took considerable manhandling and persuasion with a maul.

Although our crew could have handled it without much trouble, the Japanese had gotten into the spirit of the thing, swarming all over it at the risk of getting their fingers nipped right off.

They were a good-natured bunch, and when all was ready, the crane picked up the anchor again with chain attached and lowered it to their own deck. We heaved in on the chain. There was an anxious moment when the two ships shared the weight between them; then they had to unshackle their hold on the anchor with the awful risk of being crushed between the ships.

They managed to do it, and broke away clean. Then we heaved in on the chain until the anchor nestled into the hawse pipe without any fuss at all.

It had come home.

Anchor at the Kure Naval Museum from the battleship Mutsu, sister ship to Nagato. Photo Punynri).

SEA AND ANCHOR

Nagato's pagoda superstructure showing the damage to her
flag bridge where ADM Yamamoto heard the fateful radio call
"Tora! Tora! Tora! FADM Bill Halsey would have been pleased.
Nagato was a particular favorite target for him. Photo US Naval
Scientific Team- Japan).

We had three trial runs for the old battleship in March of
1946. Our next trial run in April, it was inevitable that we
try the anchor we had just installed, since some of the associated

gear was untested. Everything had gone well as we got steam up and performed some basic maneuvering drills in the Sagami Wan in the approaches to Yokosuka Harbor.

Captain Whipple decided to approach the anchorage from seaward in the direction of the breakwater. On the pagoda bridge, a continuous flow of reports was reaching him and his helmsman and navigation team.

"Three thousand yards to the anchorage, Sir,"

"Course to anchorage four degrees to the left, Sir."

"Estimated speed three knots, Sir."

"We seem to be set a little to the right, Sir."

"All engines stop!"

"All engines answer stopped, Sir."

Glancing over the side I could not see our speed diminishing- we were still moving along at a fair clip, from what I could observe, which is not the place you want to be at sea and anchor detail. I could feel the tension rising on the bridge.

"Distance to anchorage, eleven hundred yards, Sir."

"Right on course Sir, allowing for the set of the anchor."

"All engines back one-third!"

Captain Whipple judged that it would not do to hit the breakwater, since a collision at sea is one of those events that can spoil the whole day. The Captain was watching over the side now.

We still seemed to be making about three knots speed-of-advance, which is a practical demonstration of just how hard it is to stop a mass of forty-five thousand tons once it is set in motion. I toyed for a moment with the abstractions involved, mentally calculating momentum, mass and kinetic energy.

"Seven hundred yards to anchorage, Sir."

"All engines back full!"

"All engines answer back full, Sir!"

We could feel the deck shudder as the screws took hold. Would she stop in time? There was only one more resource to try. I noticed the cone of Fiji over the harbor, now black and sinister in the gloom. It seems we might be slowing a little, but floating objects continued to drift aft as fast as a man walks.

"Five hundred yards, Sir."

She wasn't going to stop in time.

"Two hundred yards, Sir."

"Drop anchor!"

This is what it had to be, the last chance. The ship-fitter and the boatswain's mate grappled warily with the brake wheel on the forecastle, opening it. Nothing happened. They spun it to full open. The anchor suddenly went with a rush. Straining now with the terrible intensity of men who fight for their lives, they spun the wheel back, their muscles bulging under torn shirts.

No go.

The chain roared out ever faster, striking showers of sparks as a red pall of rust rose over the forecastle. The ship was shuddering in every part. Through rifts in the dust I could make out men diving for hatches or crawling for shelter behind solid objects. We did not have much experience in our pirate crew, but they knew that as the end of the chain came thrashing out of the chain locker it would sweep the deck, pulping everything in its path.

The ship-fitter and the boatswain made a final try at the brake-wheel, then dived together headfirst down a hatch. The red pall covered the forecastle; I could get only occasional glimpses of the thumping chain. How long? The rumble of it filled the ship. There was a grunt as the bitter end came up on the chain-locker strongback, then silence.

The red cloud drifted off to starboard uncovering the crouching men. No one had been hurt.

Nagato continued to forge ahead at nearly three knots, dragging the anchor and twelve hundred feet of chain with her. But even forty-five thousand tons could not continue to transfer momentum at that rate. She began to slow, and with the breakwater looming, stopped short. The anchor buoy showed only a few yards further in than had been planned in our pre-sail meeting.

I turned to the Captain and we both smiled. "Only 2,400 miles to Bikini," I said, and remembered to breath again.

HAIRLESS JOE AND THE LONE-SOME POLECAT

When I first realized that of the twenty people in the deck force only three had appreciable sea experience, I wondered what would become of us. The decks were so vast, the gear so heavy, that it seemed we must be overwhelmed if we tried to handle her in a gale. As the days passed in Yokosuka, it sank into my consciousness that in the boatswain we had a true seaman and leader of men. Once I realized that, I was no longer apprehensive, but only curious to watch how things would work out under stress.

The boatswain was a small man, well-muscled and cat-like. One's first reaction to him might be that submerged thrill of terror the subconscious recognition of an elemental character always inspires, but it was his beard which caught the eye. Flaring straight out around his face, nowhere cut square, firm but silky, it was an ornament the like of which has not been sported since Charles V sat for his portraits. I have tried to describe the color officially. Sometimes I thought it was black with a hint of brown, sometimes brown with a hint of red, sometime mahogany, but of this I am sure – if you could get cloth of that shade it would be expensive.

It seems doubtful that the boatswain ever thought very much about himself or anything else except the situation at hand. Certainly he never weighed his words for the disconcerting effect they might produce. I shall not soon forget the day I explained to the deck force how I wanted a towing-bridle rigged. The boatswain looked up at me with all the bright-eyed benevolence of an otter appraising a proffered fish and remarked: "I didn't just understand the malarkey about frapping lines, Commander."

We then decided not to use frapping lines. Be that as it may be, his judgment was sound and he had that rare attribute of a saint or a prophet: men would follow him into any situation without question.

The boatswain's mate was a study in contrast to his Bo'sun. He was huge man, also richly muscled. A coarse black beard was trimmed close to the outlines of his massive face and he had a blank stare of an ogre out of Grimm. The Japanese lived in dread of him, and it was only after long acquaintance that I realized that for all his bulk and mien, he was only twenty-two and thought just like any other college boy, except for that one thing the war did for most young people – he no longer kidded himself. "Commander, I'm scared" he would sometimes remark as we looked over a situation.

I was genuinely sorry with a wave caught him on the fore-castle and scrubbed the anchor chain with him.

There was a rare bond of sympathy between the Bo'sun and his Mate. They were unlike other men. Each had what the other lacked. Until the sea itself forged one for us, they *were* the deck force. They kept pretty much to themselves. The pirate crew nicknamed the Bo'sun "Hairless Joe," and his hulking Mate "Lonesome Polecat."

Perhaps I should have realized what continuous failure can do even to the strongest characters. The deck force spent days rigging ladders, hanging boat booms, stringing guest-warps and knotting fenders day after day. Then a single rogue wave would sweep along *Nagato's* low freeboard and reduce them to a tangled mass of rope, wire and splinters. The disappointment took its toll upon the Bo'sun.

After all, he had his pride. He was a man-of-war sailor, used to doing things in a Navy way. The sloppy habits and un-nautical phraseology of our boots distressed him no end.

One morning muster, he simply wasn't there. The Mate and I realized at once what happened, and within a radius of a few miles where he was: in pastoral Japan, having some fascinating adventures in an alien culture without a word of Japanese to aid him.

Yokosuka Honshu-ku Train Station 1945. Photo USN.

It would have been convenient to assume he had gone to Tokyo, which was the partially correct answer. But he was not lying in some *benjo* ditch intoxicated. He had done the right thing and boarded the last train to return to the harbor, but had gone to sleep on the ride back to the Honcho-ku station and therefore missed the connecting train at Ofuna. He would not be back for a few days, since he had to thumb his way from Nagoya. The trouble was that on the evening of his disappearance the date of our sailing was advanced from eight days hence to just two, and he didn't know the new urgency that went along with his hitchhiking adventure back to the harbor in the countryside.

For our part, he was so essential to my Deck Department that it would have been unsafe to sail without him. The Eighth

Army could have picked him up for us easily enough, but that would have brought him back to *Nagato* plastered with charges and with a file of official correspondence I would have had to answer. In our extremity, recourse was had to the humble Japanese police. So the Bo'sun was restored to use on time, somewhat dazed but otherwise in good condition. I doubt whether he ever found out exactly what happened.

During the days of preparation, there had been much bantering in the bars outside the gate of the Fleet Activities- Yokosuka between men of the *Nagato* and the cruiser *Sakawa*, which would accompany us to Bikini. The latter taunted the former with being stuck on an ancient beaten-up old hulk of a dreadnaught instead of a fine modern cruiser. When the news came out from the Fleet Commander that the *Sakawa* was to sail in company with *Nagato* as junior ship in the formation, there was anguish.

This indignity was met with gnashed teeth and lamentations; why should a ship capable of making eighteen knots, with two months to spare and the world waiting, be tied to a hulk which couldn't make ten, and probably would break down at sea?

Feelings grew bitter. Later, we were to feel the effects of the bad blood.

Preparations for sea never come to an end; you keep on repairing things while other things break down until someone's blood pressure rises and the decision is reached that, ready or not, you will sail on a certain date. The pirate crew was ready mentally; they had confidence in the ship. Morale was high with everyone anxious to get away from Yokosuka. Though I had enjoyed my stay in Japan and would feel the hurt of parting, I, too, was ready to go.

On the last afternoon I managed to get away from the ship for a few hours to visit the shrine of Kamakura and see the gigantic statue of Buddha - the *Daibutsu*. The first cherry buds had burst along the path to the temple, and I felt the sense of peace that seemed to radiate from the great figure seated in the lotus position. Coming back to the waterfront, I passed the file of workmen returning from the *Nagato*.

All bowed deeply, and I gave them a salute. Then, reluctantly, I boarded a landing craft for the stinging, icy ride to the ship. As we neared her red-lead painted bulk, the grey cone of Fuji was delicately etched against the greyer sky.

Sayonara, Yoko!

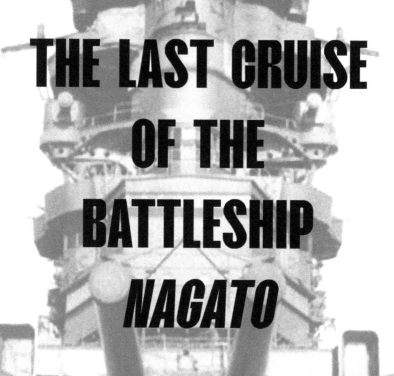

THE LAST CRUISE
OF THE
BATTLESHIP
NAGATO

Part Two:

At Sea and Underway

BIKINI BOUND

We sailed from Yokosuka amid rain squalls, slipping down the Sagami Wan by time and compass with the cruiser *Sakawa* on our port quarter. "Well begun, half done," I said to Captain Whipple. He grimaced and said he sure as hell hoped so.

The evening meal was good and movies were shown. Everyone was in high spirits. Nothing happened during the night and by morning we were clear of the land. It was a cloudy day with a gale on our port beam, but already the wind and water were warmer. We settled down into the pleasant routine of life at sea. Water was getting in through cracks and leaks everywhere, but we managed to keep ahead of it. The crew was tired but confident.

On the third day out, the wind was still abeam with rough seas, but the water was definitely bluer. It was then that we got the first hint that adventure might be in store for us.

Bridge of ex-IJN cruiser Sakawa. Photo USN.

Sakawa signaled she was making turns for fourteen knots and wondered how long she would have to keep it up. This was puzzling as we were only making ten knots, yet the two ships stayed right together. The water did seem to be slipping by pretty fast, at that. I hoped she was right. But presently the sun appeared; we shot it and it worked out. Ten knots was right.

Another message from *Sakawa*: "Fuel consumption was fantastic, there were not enough men to man the fire rooms." In short: could she slow down to eight of *her* kind of knots?

Captain Whipple directed the signal back: "Negative. *Sakawa* is junior ship and will maintain position in formation." It was ten knots through that night and the following day.

The morning of the fifth day found us in the trades with mounting deep blue seas, clear sky and wind from dead ahead. We were taking on too much water. The patch put by the Japanese on the bomb-hole in our bow was working loose and we were down a little by the head. Several pumps had failed and our electric system was in trouble as salt water reached point after hot point, shorting them out.

The crew was very tired, but the thought of doing better than *Sakawa* buoyed them up.

Finally, though, the cruiser's incessant pleas that she could not continue at that speed began to hold sway. Her Captain claimed she would be out of fuel in a few more days, and thus Captain Whipple reluctantly directed us to slow to eight knots.

The reduction hurt the fuel efficiency of the battleship and made the purchase of her rudders weaker. She became increasingly difficult to steer, her bow wandering constantly across the blue horizon.

To get the rudders deeper in the water we had to flood

compartments aft. This caused a tremor of anxiety through the crew who understood full well, despite all the sophistry of the naval vocabulary, what loss of buoyancy meant. Water foamed in over the seacocks. We began to bail.

Morale of the crew rose again the next day as we prepared to take *Sakawa* in tow when she actually ran out of fuel. Now, they would show those people who had the better ship!

The towing wire was too heavy for our small deck force to handle in the usual way. We could call on the larger force of engineers when absolutely necessary, but only for short periods since they had boilers to tend. We took a couple turns of towing wire around the number four turret and led it aft to a pelican hook for quick release should anything go wrong. Then we cut through the port-towing hook, dragging it forward. It was tough dirty work, keeping the weight always on the deck. We hung loops over the side and made them fast with light hemp lines.

The idea was that *Sakawa* would pull the towing wire off us gradually, breaking the hemp lines one by one, as a man might pull an adhesive plaster off his chest. Working up to a position amidships on the port side we lashed down a bight and carried the wire aft again the same way but with different hemp lines, then around the stern and forward on the starboard side nearly to the bow.

From the end of the wire we continued with six hundred feet of eight-inch hawser, lashing it in place the same way, and continued that with three-inch and finally one-inch line terminating in a float.

The plan was that we would float the small line back to *Sakawa*; then we would haul the three-inch and the eight-inch lines in as we cut away the hemp lines—then the cruiser would take a strain on the eight-inch with her winch and pull the eye of the towing wire over and make flat to it, and then pull off the full length of the towing wire.

Hairless Joe the Bo'sun would follow along with a fire axe, just in case anything got stuck.

It didn't work that way the first time, but *Sakawa* managed to raise steam and we proceeded south, making best speed possible. We had no idea how much fuel we had, or what tanks really contained seawater. This was something quite unlike anything I had ever seen at sea, and we were not even half-way to the Marshall Islands.

FUEL STATE CRITICAL

Ex-IJN Nagato making steam at her Yokosuka anchorage to get underway for the Marshall islands. Alongside her is the Tank lighter that served as her link to shore. Colorized photo USN.

As we accomplished the rig, the weather became very clear and warm with the seas rising higher and bluer in hue. Occasionally a rogue wave would board us. We had to be constantly alert on the deck to ensure none of the Deck Force was swept overboard. Both ships were now having trouble with electrical failures. The fuel tanks were yielding increasing quantities of salt water; first one ship and then the other would have to stop as the fires under the boilers were drowned out.

From the flood of messages flying between the battleship and the cruiser, it was evident that neither ship knew how much oil she had left, nor how much of that she could have got. It still seemed possible that *Nagato* had enough to make port with *Sakawa* in tow. At least that was the situation the next brilliant dawn as *Sakawa* began to yaw widely and then went DIW - dead in the water - beam on to the sea.

At first she would not admit it was anything more serious that what had occurred before. We hovered around all morning, burning precious fuel, waiting for her to raise steam. Then she admitted she could go no further and we maneuvered to attempt to take her in tow again.

She picked the small line up as planned, but the crew of *Sakawa* really did not want that tow. Somehow or other, their combined effort was insufficient to lift the eight-inch hawser on deck. A stalemate developed as daylight passed. We signaled her to cast off. She did so.

With that, Captain Whipple decided to walk right up to them and practically hand them the eight-inch line. Every man we could possibly be spared from his post was there to watch. Up to that moment, *Sakawa* had seemed a small grey thing by day and a cluster of lights by night; but we began to realize how big she really was; how heavily she tossed on the seas.

We would see light under the first fifty feet of her bow and then her stern would rise out of the water, falling back down with an audible thud and spurts of foam. As we came up from astern, the wind brought down the sound of the whine of her blowers. It was a tense moment as the Gunner stood up to put a shot-line across.

Every man aboard must have felt a thrill of terror. We were within two hundred feet of her when the gun banged. They got the line and then lost it. We circled and came in even closer, tossing them a line by hand. They lost that one, too. The third try we came very close. *Sakawa's* bow was deflected toward us on the crest of a huge swell. For a moment it hung over our forecastle like a meat cleaver and I thought the cruise would end right there, but a swell heaved up in between the hulls, forcing the bows apart.

The next wave threw *Sakawa's* stern our way and crushed into us amidships. Later, I dove to see the hole. You could have driven a truck through it. We sank a little lower in the water and our starboard list increased from three to five degrees.

But Captain Whipple was putting a line aboard the *Sakawa* that day, damn the consequences. He came in again. The crew of *Sakawa* may have had the impression that it was either get the line aboard or finish the voyage in *Nagato.* Anyway, they got it this time, and began to peel the towing wire from our side as planned. Then our difficulties really began.

The wire caught on obstructions from *Nagato's* massive flank. Hairless Joe had a field day with the fire axe. Sailors, watching for their chance, clambered over the side to free the tow wire, held to the ship by light lines or perhaps only by one foot, waves dashing completely over them. Slowly we cleared the wire aft clear to the stern.

Now came a new difficulty. *Sakawa* could not veer out to our port quarter to peel the line; she had to tug at it from dead astern. The boatswain with his fire axe was joined by the Shipfitter with an acetylene torch glowing white hot at the tip. They cut away obstructions one by one. It was slow but hopeful work. Perhaps we would succeed after all.

Then misfortune overtook us. *Sawaka* bucked on the crest of a sea, the wire tightened, carrying away the rest of the help lines, the bight amidships lashed high in the air to settle in a running knot on a pair of bits. It seemed impossible it could even be got off.

We were well and truly in a pickle, and we had no idea how to save the day.

I called RM2 Herschler to the Bridge and told him to make radio contact with the Naval base in Eniwetok, some 200 miles away, and request immediate assistance.

He did, and they advised they would send two navy tugs to our aid.

NAGATO ADRIFT

We eventually got the tow-wire un-fouled from the turret with great difficulty. Hairless Joe the Bo'sun, his Mate the Lonesome Polecat, the Shipfitter and the First Lieutenant worked out onto the wave-swept blister, clutching at the overhead as swells hissed past. They rigged a chainfall and heaved round. It took more than an hour, since the men could work only during the momentary lull between the sweep off water across the deck.

The sun was till an hour high when the wire slipped off the

last obstruction and sank. We held our breath at the *Sakawa* took the strain. The wire snapped out of the water, came taut, and then relaxed.

We had her in tow, just as planned.

Not for long, however. A lumpy blue hill heaved up between the ships. *Sakawa* reared back like a frightened horse. There was a flash and a bang on the fantail as puffs of rust and fragments of wire flew everywhere. Failure again. We stopped in our tracks, sat down, sunk in apathy.

I roused myself to admire the sunset: gorgeous orange spangles on the azure hills. Something caught in the corner of my eye. The towing wire was not hanging straight down from the bow of the *Sakawa*, it tended forward and seemed to be jerking a little. Incredible! But we really were still fast to her.

When the wire broke, the pelican hook had caught in the port towing check. We lashed it down with many turns of wire rope. *Sakawa* fell into position astern of us, in tow as planned. As the crew filed off to the galley, spray coming aboard was violet in the fading light. They had worked mightily through a day of danger, frustration and failure, to win. I hope they would get a good night's sleep.

And then of course it was time for the Number 7 boiler to explode with a great muffled blast and a cloud of black smoke from the stack. We were now left without propulsion and electrical power, which meant no cooking facilities. Their lighting below deck was solely from flashlights, and our food sources were K and C rations. Drinking water was rationed, and despite the labors of the Deck Department, I could only let them could only drink at certain times of the day.

The water rose high enough in the ship causing the bilge rats to surface and run freely down the halls. They were particularly active at night, and the "rat race" amid the general stench was unnerving.

In the early morning hours, I was wakened with the order to get out a sea anchor. Why? *The engines were about to stop.*

Call all hands! *General Quarters!*

We didn't have a sea anchor in the inventory. The electricians rigged floodlights on the forecastles. On an eight-inch hawser longer than the ship, we rigged something like the tail of a boy's kite. Cargo nets, spars, long festoons of Japanese canvas, and iron bars at intervals so it would sink. It worked.

As the engines ground dismally to a stop, the ship's head held up to the seas. Without the anchor, she would have had the weather on her port quarter, and much more brine than we could have handled would have come aboard, perhaps causing us to founder and sink right there.

When writing out the watch-bills in Yokosuka, I took care to reserve the dawn watch, from four to eight, to myself. That is one of the perquisites of being senior watch officer, and I took it happily. In my mind, these are the best hours of the day at sea; the splendor of the night, the miracle of dawn, breakfast, and a cup of hot coffee all in four hours.

It was then time then to go through the ceremony of relieving the watch.

With the ship dying under him, the only thing the Officer of the Deck could do was call the Captain who could give orders to the *Sakawa* which she probably could not obey.

She was showing the lights of a vessel being towed. As the first grey of dawn etched in her lines against blackness, it was evident that the weight of the towing wire sinking down into the depths was drawing the ships together. Presently the weight would cause us to collide; and if *that* situation were allowed to continue, in time both would sink. Without sufficient life rafts, we would likely drown before help could arrive.

Soon I could make out men working on *Sakawa's* forecastle. Fifty or more of them tagging on a line got enough slack to unshackle our wire. They cast it off. In a dying effort, the *Sakawa* managed a few turns of one screw. That carried her clear and she dropped lifeless into the trough of the sea.

Standing on the bridge as the sun rose, I watched the crew of *Nagato* climb wearily up into the superstructure and go to sleep there. There was nothing more they could do. The ship wallowed idly to the sea anchor, taking water, but not enough to worry about. The warmth of the sun felt good.

At noon, K rations were broken out and the men brought fresh water up to the deck in pails. Down below, the interior spaces seemed vast in the feeble rays of my flashlight. Water was dripping everywhere. That was the only sound. The gloom and the sound of falling water reminded me of being in the limestone caves of Kentucky.

Up in the forepeak, dimly lit by shafts of daylight from ports and hatches, one could hear the slap of waves against the bow while the whole structure creaked and groaned. With no power to operate machinery, it sounded exactly like the forepeak of a man o' war must have sounded from the days of sail.

By later afternoon the resilience of youth brought the men out to amuse themselves on deck. Nor did they lack for subject matter. Sharks came drifting in out of the blue to circle the lifeless hulk. From the foremast we could see them first as olive-green blotches far below the surface. Ever circling, very slowly, they drew into the sunlit transparency about us until every detail of their fins and gills were visible; theirs was the deadly certainty of those who knew they have only to wait. They would take anything that was offered. We could hear the jaws snap as they closed on a loaf of bread. The boys hooked some and shot others, but never got one on deck. They were too big for that.

The second day an albatross came skimming in close to the

water, robbing power from the waves as a surfboarder does until he has enough to shoot up over the mast and hover there. Just as I expected, someone fired at him. It seems the birds have learned something from the war; anyway, this one ducked and came in a little later to strafe the deck, scoring two hits on personnel. Soon he was joined by others of his species. They stayed with us till landfall, enjoying the free ride. They could not have been omens, could they?

DECK DIVISION

Late in the afternoon of March 30th a speck was seen on the horizon. A tug had found us! It took *Sakawa* in tow, and then slowly vanished over the blue disk of the horizon. Another tug appeared before midnight.

I was glad the Captain told her to lie off until morning. When the sun was an hour high, we tried first to fuel from her. All hands were ready with spars weighted at the butt with pieces of iron, and each with a light line lashed to the smaller end. As the tug closed amidships, we thrust them in between; they saved her from destruction for our massive side. A hose was passed without difficulty and we began to take oil.

But the spar only lasted a few minutes; almost every roll of the tug splintered one. It became like a production operation: men on the hangar deck brought new spars out and cut notches in them with axes, other men fastened lines and weights, men on the blister thrust them in between, while still other men retrieved lines from splintered stumps. Meanwhile, we finally realized it was only a question of time before a larger swell crushed her against us in spite of the spars. After we had a few thousand gallons, she knocked off fueling and prepared to take us in tow.

USS Clamp, ARS-33. Photo USN.

Before that could be done, we had to get the sea anchor in. It was a Herculean task – the temptation to slip the sea anchor was great, but we might need it again. The last impediment came off late that afternoon. Then, with no steam to work the winch, we had to call all hands to get the tug's wires aboard. Before sunset she had taken the strain and we seemed to be making three knots due south towards our destination in the Marshall Islands. The crew turned in for what was supposed to be a night's sleep.

Towards midnight a larger tug- USS *Clamp* (ARS-33) showed up. Her skipper didn't want to tow in tandem so we had to call all hands to take the strain off the small tug's wire while we unshackled. She went astern of us to await further orders. We sat on the forecastle, waiting under the stars. The ship's battery had revived enough to supply the feeble floodlights, but they were turned out.

Only the barely audible sobbing of the wind was to be heard. The red riding light of the larger tug was just visible off to starboard. Slowly, it brightened until we picked up the muffled singsong of her engines.

Then she seemed to burst upon us out of the night, her floodlit fantail alive with barebacked, sweating men, blazing away with line throwing guns.

Our men ducked warily behind bits and winches, for the line-throwing slug weighs half a pound and can deal a vicious blow. The light threads they carried over were lost in the darkness; we could not find them. The tug passed under our bow, circled, and came in again, still firing.

One of our crew caught a thread well aft. Fifty men were upon it like demons. The deck thudded as they pressed forward in a whirling mob, keeping pace with the tug. A heavier line came singing over as they reached our bow; they whisked it through the check, raced aft; in less than ten seconds a three-inch line was aboard. Others milling in the bow seized on that, made off with it, streaking aft. An eight-inch line came aboard.

Men came racing from everywhere to heave in on it. The tug was back down under our bow. All hands were straining on the eight-inch in the yellow glow of the floodlights; it eased in steadily until the eye of the wire came in through the check to the Bo'sun waiting with his heavy steel pin to shackle on. No one had to give an order; it was teamwork, concentrated energy, the will to win. It confirmed what I had realized for several days: we now had a real professional deck force.

Climbing up to relieve the watch, I reviewed the steps by which this had come about. The original members of the deck forces were not much better than they had been; a little smarter, a little more muscular, perhaps, but still drudges.

This new strength of the team came from men not normally rated to be deck people at all. The case of a signalman flashed through my mind as a series of vivid pictures. I noticed him first as we were preparing to tow, watching intently from the signal bridge.

By the time we had worked up forward, he was down to the hurricane deck, still watching. As we passed lines between the ships, he mingled with the deck force, diffident and uncertain, but heaving round every time he got the chance.

During the dangerous operation of freeing the wire, I saw him hanging over the edge of the wave-swept blister, easing it over an obstruction while two other men held him by the foot. From there on, he was always in the thick of things. A middle-aged Chief, constrained to paper-pushing administrative work those many years, plunged in like an eighteen-year-old.

One of the shipfitters took his place right behind the Bo'sun and stayed there.

So it was: cooks, an alleged steward, radio men, messmen, a storekeeper, learned as I watched down from the pagoda, until I could call "all hands on deck!" and relax, completely confident. It was the American spirit, plus the leader on the deck, the Bo'sun. It was an unbeatable combination.

Next morning we fueled again from the smaller tug, but not alongside this time. The plan was for her to steam close in on our starboard quarter where we would pass her a hose lashed to a three-inch line.

The first try almost cancelled the idea. The tug got in position all right, then came careening down the slope of a great swell, putting her anchor through a splinter shield with a ringing crash. The steel was twisted and torn with the clean forty-five-degree fracture one normally associates with the detonation of high explosives. Then she went lurching up our side, carrying away booms, davits, stanchions, safety lines and all her own beading, and taking several gashes in her wooden hull, none of them clear though.

She got clear in no danger of sinking, and regained position. We passed the hose. It worked this time, and black oil was soon bubbling into our tanks. Once or twice the hose burst, spraying us with Diesel Fuel-Marine (DFM), but new sections were quickly substituted for the torn ones.

The trouble was the great labor of handling the hose. It was a big job. The tug could not keep station accurately, ranging ahead and behind, in and out. Our men had to pay out hose as she bore away, take it in smartly as she came back, keeping it out of the water where the waves might tear it loose. Thirty men were barely enough to do it, and they lasted only a little while before they were exhausted and had to be relieved. We kept that up all day, changing the watch once an hour. We had our reward; by nightfall, steam had been raised and lights and pumps were going again.

Next morning, land was sighted from the foretop, only to be lost to view as the wind freshened and the tug could no longer hold our head to the seas. By noon we were back; by late afternoon we could make out ships in the anchorage.

Then we received an extraordinary message. Just after sunset, I went out on the forecastle and told the leading petty officer to take all the men he could find and close ports, hatches, and watertight doors, working back inside the armor, taking all the men with him. He looked at me with question marks in his eyes. I told him I really was crazy just as he had always thought, but to go ahead and do it anyway.

He did.

Later I learned that his theory was that I knew the collision with a reef was inevitable. Actually, the message was from the Fleet Commander's weather-guesser, and it informed us that a tidal wave- a tsunami- might be coming our way, and to take precautions.

The tug had reversed course and was trying to get us to deep water where we would have a better chance, though she might not. It was too hot to keep the men inside the armor citadel very long; we let them come out on one of the upper decks aft of the pagoda, hoping to see the wave in time to get them undercover. I wanted the Captain to run up the Dutch Ensign as a signal to drop the anchor, but he wouldn't.

Nothing happened through the night. The next morning, we found ourselves 30 miles out to sea facing another day of tugboats, broken tow-lines, power failures and a bunch of upset sailors. Though we never felt the effect of the tidal wave where thousands of Hawaiians were made homeless, we did manage to drop the anchor in Eniwetok on April 4th, the 18th day of the voyage, sporting a drunken seven-degree list to port.

Now in safe anchorage, we could start pumping *Nagato* out, fix her boilers, and prepare for the last 200 miles to Bikini. And our date with The Atom Bomb.

MUTINY IN PARADISE

Laura Beach on Eniwetok, Marshall Islands. Photo Wiki.

By mid-morning on the 4th of April, 1946, we had channel fever and decided that the threat posed by a gigantic rogue wave - a tsunami - had passed. We entered the lagoon at Eniwetok Atoll under tow via the deep-water channel north of Parry Island. We were sporting a rakish seven-degree list to port and poor *Nagato* looked quite the worse for wear.

It was a relief to drop the anchor and secure the deck

department for some much needed rest as we prepared to have workboats alongside to begin emergency pumping. We had hundreds of tons of seawater in compartments fore and aft; the former had flooded due to existing battle damage, and the latter a product of the counter-flooding aft we had to do to maintain steerage.

It was a relief to have a chance to relax a bit and look around. The Crossroads tests were scheduled for July, and with much fanfare, but I considered we would be ready in plenty of time to make our appointment with the atom bombs. We had several pleasant uneventful weeks there. On board we patched up boilers; the sailors went ashore and I spent most of my time with fins and a mask, exploring the coral reefs. Eniwetok Atoll, for which the whole aggregation of 40 islands is named, is home to 850 native Marshall Islanders.

In terms of land area, the whole sprawling chain is only a couple square miles of dry land *in toto*, and no part of it is more than fifteen feet in elevation. We were only about 190 nautical miles from our destination at Bikini, which had been selected as the optimal location for the Operation Crossroads Atomic test series for which *Nagato* was going to play a starring role.

We were determined to make it under our own power, and in watching the Bo'sun forge the deck department into a can-do unit, I was confident we could do it, if we could have a few weeks to pump out and conduct some basic repairs to the boilers and take on a reliable quantity of diesel fuel.

The atoll had a curious history. It had passed from Spanish

to German control by the time of the First War and had been occupied by the Empire of Japan along with the rest of the Marshalls in 1914. That possession was formalized by the League of Nations in 1920, and was administered as the Japanese South Pacific Mandate. As part of the buildup for the Pacific War, the Japs built an airfield on Engebi Island, which they used as an emergency strip to refuel planes flying between the big Japanese naval complex at Truk and the islands to the east.

Eniwetok was reinforced in 1944 with a few thousand troops from the Imperial Army's 1st Amphibious Brigade, which had served in China. The Japs were not able to complete their defensive works on the beaches, and were not ready for the five-day American invasion in February of 1944. Most of the major combat occurred on Engebi Islet, the most important Japanese installation on the atoll. Combat also occurred on the main islet of Eniwetok itself and on Parry Island, where the Japanese had constructed a seaplane base.

Following its capture, the anchorage at Eniwetok became a major forward Fleet operating base as we leap-frogged toward the Philippines around the still-occupied Japanese islands, cutting them off and letting their garrisons starve.

When the atoll was a going logistics concern in July of 1944, the daily average number of ships in the lagoon was 488. That shows you what the impact of war production was, since that number is a hundred more than there were ships in the entire US Navy Fleet in 1941.

The total tumbled as the war swept west and north, and

now there was a curious sense of abandonment. There were Quonset huts to accommodate the throngs of sailors and airmen who had been here in 1944, and now the runways, repair shops fuel farms, hardstands, hospitals, marine railway and floating pipeline gave the place an eerie sense of abandonment. Only a token garrison on Eniwetok was left, and the outlying facilities were left just as they were in 1945.

The natives seemed phlegmatic about the amazing storm that had passed over and through them. In several instances bunkers and the like are now used as sheds and pigsties, and larger structures, such as air command centers or ammunitions depots, were used for human habitation. The Japanese radio-direction finding and command building on Taroa Island was being used to hold worship services, a holy purpose for a structure built as part of the war machine of the Empire of the Sun.

Our former companion-ship *Sakawa* had arrived long before we did, and as our crew cycled ashore, we began to hear just how bad the blood was between our two ships.

The actual events of the cruise south from Yokosuka had been curiously inverted. In one version of the sea-story heard at the Officer's and Enlisted Club on Eniwetok, it was *Sakawa* who had come to the assistance of *Nagato*, and attempted to rescue her senior partner.

We discovered that a Liberty Ship tanker, the *Nickajack Trail*, had been diverted to bring us fuel while we were adrift and dead in the water, but had run aground in bad weather and been lost.

USS Nickajack Trail - Japtan Island

Sakawa had something else we did not have: eleven of her former Japanese officers aboard to assist the American crew. I don't know if some of the Japanese pride had affected them, but there were obviously some significant morale problems that did not affect the pirate crew of our battleship.

It is often said that the United States Navy has never had a mutiny, and since *Sakawa* had no standing on anyone's naval register, that may still be true. But we did discover at Eniwetok that it was not for lack of trying.

The story emerged that five of the ship's American sailors were angry over the dismal working conditions aboard *Sakawa*. In a ship normally staffed by over 730 men, the Navy had assigned a crew of only 165. *Nagato* only had 180, but the enormous amount of work required by all hands just made us more determined.

Not so on *Sakawa*. The five sailors decided that they were not going to Bikini, or anywhere else, and removed the pressure line to the over-speed trip valves in the fuel system to sabotage the ship, and then poured sand into the oil and water pumps. They smashed gauges, tachometers, and cut high pressure steam lines in an attempt to get relieved of duty aboard the bedraggled cruiser.

Rather than being relieved of duty as they had hoped, the five sailors were brought up on charges. I credit Captain Whipple's steady, firm leadership for the lack of such profound discipline problems on *his* battleship.

Editor's note: Machinery sabotage is not unknown in Navy annals, and turmoil on the mess decks was noted with some frequency in the Vietnam conflict.

After three weeks of repairs on Eniwetok, flooded compartments pumped out and repairs performed on the most critical machinery, we were ready to depart for Bikini and *Nagato's* last mission.

As we got underway on our own power on the 25th of April, we discovered that the old lady seemed to want to show her stuff for this final sprint. The great monster managed to cruise at 13 knots, the best speed we ever got out of her.

We made the trip alone without any help and managed to drop the anchor at our assigned spot all by ourselves. We made it in two days, down to one serviceable boiler, but she answered all bells right until we made fast to our assigned buoy.

That would be the last time she moved on her own power, but we did not know that. We assumed that after the tests we would have to get underway again for destinations unknown.

Sakawa did not make it to Bikini Atoll until May. In addition to repairing the sabotaged machinery, they had to take time to conduct five individual Captain's Masts.

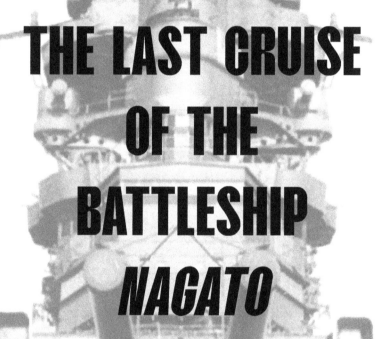

THE LAST CRUISE
OF THE
BATTLESHIP
NAGATO

Part Three:
Able, Baker and Charlie

TESTING, ONE, TWO THREE...

VADM "Spike" Blandy, Commander, Joint Task force ONE

"The bomb will not start a chain-reaction in the water converting it all to gas and letting the ships on all the oceans drop down to the bottom. It will not blow out the bottom of the sea and let all the water run down the hole. It will not destroy gravity. I am not an atomic playboy, as one of my critics labeled me, exploding these bombs to satisfy my personal whim."

– Vice Admiral W.H.P. Blandy, Commander Joint
Task Force One, Operation Crossroads

You could argue that when the hook went down at Bikini, our job was pretty much done. We would be supporting the tests of the Atom Bomb on our target ship, of course, but it was Washington that was running this show in the placid and peaceful waters of Bikini Atoll.

Moray eel. Image courtesy Wikipedia.

It was quite remarkable. Scientists swarmed aboard fitting us out with instruments to measure the effects of the atomic bomb on the ship. It was best to stay out of their way, so I found a flat-topped coral head with a foot of water over it at low tide. The work-boat dropped me off there every morning on its way to the beach and picked me up on its way back three or four hours later. This paradise I shared with a moray eel. I never saw all of him but his neck was as thick as the upper part of my leg.

I had a harpoon and probably could have taken him in a fight but though he watched me carefully, gulping in a meditative way, he never made a move to attack.

Of course, if he had any idea what we were going to do to that coral head he called home he might better have been advised to do so. As would I, and the rest of my shipmates. There was no particular reason for us to know what was going on. We all knew that the use of the two bombs against Hiroshima and Nagasaki had eliminated the grim necessity for a massive invasion of the Home Islands, and one could argue that it was the astonishing nature of the Bombs that gave the proud Japanese the ability to throw in the towel with honor.

Certainly a lot of us would have been killed, and more of *them*.

I knew that for a cold hard fact. I had visited the Imperial Naval station at Saesebo on the island of Kyushu as part of my assignment with NavTechJap, which was the abbreviated designation for the US Naval Technical Mission to Japan. We reported to Captain C.G. Grimes, who had been Fleet Intelligence Officer in charge of Technical Assessment at the Joint Intelligence Center - Pacific Ocean Area (JICPOA) in Hawaii during the war. He was charged with collecting the essential elements of information contained in the intelligence annex for Operation BLACKLIST, the secret plan for the Occupation of Japan.

It was secret for a good reason. The invasion of Kyushu was termed "Operation OLYMPIC," which would have been followed by "Operation CORONET" on the island of Honshu. Both were expected to go on for months, but BLACKLIST provided for contingency operations in the event of a sudden capitulation of the militarists. In light of the effect of the Atom Bombs, that is precisely what happened, and Captain Grimes was designated Chief of Mission.

Sasebo was just north of Omua Bay, on which the city of Nagasaki was located, so it was not hard to appreciate the magnitude of the power unleashed on the city. Sasebo had been one of the finalists for the honor of the Atomic demonstration, something that did not pass without comment when we visited.

I have always been amazed that the two bombs dropped on Japan were only the second and third times the technology had been attempted. Many of the technicians who swarmed aboard *Nagato* had been at the first one, the Trinity test on the Alamogordo weapons range in New Mexico. When we detonated the next two in the air above the two cities we really did not have much of an idea about what their effects were going to be, except that we knew it was going to be huge. There was no way to really understand how these things worked and what they did except to take the time, now that we had it, to understand it.

The chain of events that ended the war came with incredible speed. In the New Mexico desert on 16 July 1945, scientists of the Manhattan District secretly carried out the "Trinity Test" with the first explosion of the atomic bomb. On 5 August, only three weeks after this test, the first military atomic bomb exploded over Hiroshima, and a few days later another atomic bomb exploded over Nagasaki. The Japanese made their unconditional surrender on 14 August, nine days after the A-Bombs had been dropped.

Even before technical personnel made their studies in Japan, reports of the damage at Hiroshima and Nagasaki offered conclusive proof of the tremendous military potential of the new weapon.

The CROSSROADS series were intended to scientifically measure the precise effects of the Atom Bomb, and how it might be used in a military context. I can only assume that it was also a statement to potential rivals, since there was immense radio and press coverage of the events, but it was not the business of a deck officer to worry about that.

The CROSSROADS series was intended to be a three-event series, covering the second half of 1946 and the beginning of 1947. The first ("ABLE") was to be an air-dropped weapon, similar to one of the two used on Japan. The second ("BAKER") would be detonated in relatively shallow water, and the third ("CHARLIE") was programmed to be exploded deep at the bottom of Bikini's lagoon.

There was so much that we didn't know about how these instruments of infernal power worked. The only closely observed explosion had been at Trinity, which was still officially a secret. Some of the scientists did talk about it, though it was only later that some of the details came out. That such small things could produce such large explosions was still hard to conceptualize.

Years later I saw a picture of the fissionable core of the Trinity device, a thing they called "The Gadget."

Sgt. Herbert Lehr delivering the plutonium core for the Gadget in its shock-mounted carrying case to the assembly room in the McDonald Ranch House at the Alamogordo test site. Photo U.S. Government/AEC)

July 16, 1945: 05:29:45 Mountain War Time, Trinity Site, Alamogordo Test Range, Jornada del Muerto desert. Yield: 19 – 21 Kilotons. Photo US Government/AEC.

Finding out what these things could really do is precisely why we were ordered to take Japan's last battleship to this lovely lagoon, where the diving amid the teaming undersea life was indeed extraordinary.

BETWEEN DOOMSDAY AND THE 4TH OF JULY

Ex-Prinz Eugen in the lagoon at Bikini. Photo USN.

The Navy Brass wanted to compare and contrast the survivability of both American and Axis ships, which is why the Nazi Hipper-class heavy Cruiser *Prinz Eugen* was brought all the way from Europe for the test. By the time she arrived at Bikini, she was officially known as USS *IX 300*, which is the oddest ship name I have seen in my time in the Navy. I have to say she was a handsome ship when I saw her riding at anchor.

I got plenty of swimming and snorkeling in the lagoon near

the big coral head with my associate, the enormous Moray Eel during the three weeks that passed between our arrival and the test. The lagoon was bustling with activity, just as it had been when the Pacific War swept over this usually placid place.

Nagato was part of a fleet of target ships, anchored with military precision near Bikini Island at the eastern end of the vast lagoon. The center of the formation was USS *Nevada,* the proud survivor of the attack on Pearl Harbor whose services were not longer needed.

It was a little strange to be casually throwing away such powerful ships, but I have always believed that men o' war are nothing more than smelted iron oxide trying- successfully- to return to that natural state.

There was a practical reality, too. The Navy Department had a whole fleet of new ships and the old ones were going to either be decommissioned or discarded, or they would break the bank in trying to maintain them in operational condition. So, away they would go.

Ninety-five ships were designated as targets for the ABLE blast. In addition to our little Japanese convoy, and *Prinz Eugen*, there were four USN battleships, two aircraft carriers, a brace of cruisers, eleven Destroyers, eight Fleet submarines and a host of auxiliaries and amphibious craft. Some of the latter were beached to demonstrate the effect of atomic blast on a simulated landing force. All the ships were laden with sample amounts of fuel and ammunition, plus scientific instruments to measure air pressure, ship's movement, and radiation.

We read in the newspapers that eventually made it out to the lagoon that there were complaints about the live animals that had been brought out to ride the ships during the tests. I had not heard of "humane activists" for animals before, but obviously we could not ask American sailors to be exposed to the blast, and an acceptable substitute was deemed to be a few hundred pigs, guineas pigs, goats, rats, mice and insects to be placed on the target ships.

Some of the goats had their fur shaved to present a more human-like hairless surface. Some of the pigs were even equipped with their own "flash Suits" like the ones the Navy had developed for shipboard use to evaluate their effectiveness.

All this was supported by a surface force of more than 150 ships that provided quarters, experimental stations, and workshops for most of the 42,000 Army and Navy personnel. Navy made up the vast majority of the Joint Task Force (37,000) and we had 37 female Navy Nurses, a ratio that worked out to one lady for each one thousand sailors.

You can bet they were pretty popular!

The story of inter-service rivalry was a long standing impediment to Joint Operations. The creation of the Air Force from Army Air Corps was based on the contention that the Air Force could deliver the A-Bomb anywhere. Army and Navy each held seats in the Cabinet. The war in the Pacific was fought in two components due to sensitivities between the staffs of Nimitz and MacArthur. A more complete discussion of CROSSROADS in this context helps underpin some of the observations in Ed Gilfillen's account.

Additional personnel were located on nearby atolls such as Eniwetok, where we had our repairs done, and Kwajalein. It was a big operation, and most everyone felt it was an honor to be part of it.

Navy personnel were allowed to extend their service obligation for one year if they wanted to participate in the tests and see an atomic bomb explode. The papers back home were promoting this as being something between Doomsday and the Fourth of July celebration.

B-17s and B-29s roared over the lagoon in practice formations for the test. Gallant old Nevada was painted a bright red with her gun tubes painted a bright white in order to give the Air Corps bombardier the best target presentation.

Around her, at the center of the target cluster, the density was 20 ships per square mile, which in my experience was three or four times greater than what combat doctrine would recommend. The stated goal was not to duplicate a realistic anchorage, but to measure damage as a function of distance from the blast center, at as many different distances as possible.

The arrangement also reflected the outcome of the Army/ Navy disagreement about how many ships should be allowed to sink, which was part of the underlying inter-service rivalry that was bubbling fiercely over what roles the Military Departments would have in the Atomic Age.

There were even some people that thought there should be a completely new service created out of the Air Corps, intended to deliver the A-bomb anywhere on earth.

I saw some of the combat art that was created as part of the big publicity coverage of the event. LCDR Art Beaumont did an oil painting of us being evacuated from the ships the afternoon before the ABLE test was designated a "go" for the first of July, 1946.

We abandoned *Nagato* to her fate late on the afternoon of the 30th of June. I patted her heavy steel flank as we clambered down the ladder to board landing craft of the support fleet.

The utility craft in turn took us to safe positions on transports stationed a minimum of ten nautical miles east of the atoll. We were issued special dark glasses or goggles to protect our eyes, but a decision was made shortly before ABLE that the glasses might not be adequate. The final guidance from on high was that we should turn away from the blast, shut our eyes, and cradle our face in the crook of our elbows for additional protection.

And that was the way it was in that lovely lagoon the night

before the power of the Atom was going to be demonstrated against my own ship. Well, it was a borrowed ship, but my ship, nonetheless. I wondered if I would see her again. Captain Whipple seemed to be confident that we would.

I wondered when I would be able to go snorkeling again, and what the Moray Eel was going to think about the whole affair.

We would not have long to wait. The word was passed that we could expect H-hour to be at nine local time - 2100 GMT. In the official history, they changed the term for the moment of detonation to "Mike" hour. I guess they thought that "How-Hour," which is the way we said it phonetically, made the whole thing seem a little silly.

USS Nevada (BB- 36) was painted bright orange to assist the B-29 bomber crew find their aim point for the first atomic test of Operation CROSSROADS. This view was painted from life by combat Artist LCDR Art Beaumont from the bridge of USS Arkansas (BB-33). Nagato's unique pagoda superstructure is visible behind her bow.

SITUATION (AB)NORMAL

Hollywood Bombshell Rita Hayworth in her 1946 role of "Gilda."
The Fat Man A-Bomb used for the ABLE test at Bikini was
named for her and her likeness was stenciled on the weapon
prior to M-hour.

We abandoned ship just before the bomb dropped for Test
ABLE and were back on *Nagato* a day later. We were taken
by landing craft to the observation anchorage some ten miles
east of the center of the target ship anchorage centered around
the battleship Nevada in her merry red paint.

We rose early on ABLE Day to await M-hour. We were supposed to be ready for the greatest demonstration of raw destructive power in the world's history.

The type bomb, I learned later, was one of the "Fat Man" implosion bomb designs that had been used at Nagasaki. The press was having a field day with the Public Affairs staff of Joint Task Force ONE under Rear Admiral Blandy. The bomb itself had been named after an actress who was termed a bombshell herself. Rita Hayworth played a character named "Gilda" in the Hollywood movie of the same name that summer.

Gilda's A-Bomb
Probably the greatest publicity break any picture or any star ever received was Columbia's "Gilda," with Rita Hayworth, because of the A-Bomb plant that hit every news story yesterday and the day before and every broadcast of the Bikini happenings. This break is a cinch to add at least a million to the probable $5,000,000 domestic gross on the show.

Prior to dawn, preparations were in progress on the support ships all over the task force and at air bases on the atolls in the region. Eight B-17 Flying Fortress bombers had been modified with radio-controlled autopilots, converting them into remotely controlled loaded with automatic cameras, radiation detectors, and air sample collectors.

Being un-manned, the Forts could fly into radiation environments, such as the mushroom-shaped cloud that the ABLE blast would produce. It was assumed that such exposure would be fatal to human aircrew.

All the land-based detonation-sequence photographs were taken by remote control from tall lattice-based towers erected on several islands of the atoll. In all, the Public Affairs people had announced that the Bikini cameras would take 50,000 still pictures and a million and a half feet of high-speed motion picture film.

GILDA was going to be dropped from Superfortress B-29-40-MO #4427354 from the 509th Bombardment Wing. That was the elite successor Wing to the Roswell, New Mexico-based unit that had conducted the atomic bombings of Japan. "Dave's Dream" had in fact been at Nagasaki, then named "Big Stink."

Under that nose-art the aircraft had an admirable operational record, being flown by the greatest number of crews assigned to the mission. She was renamed for the CROSSROADS mission in honor of Captain David Semple, a 509th bombardier who had been killed in a crash that year.

For ABLE, the pilot would be Major Woodrow Swancutt, assisted by Copilot Captain William C. Harrison, and Bombardier Major Harold H. Wood. All the moving parts were headed in the right direction, and on the observation ships emotion and interest were rising.

In the final minutes before the drop, we heard the call to make preparations to protect our eyes, either by turning away, holding our arms over our faces or wearing special goggles. There was not a man among us who did not want to see the dawn of a new age for ourselves.

And that is precisely when the SNAFU began. Situation Normal, all F**ked Up.

GILDA detonated 520 feet above the target fleet, with a yield of 23 kilotons. Five ships were sunk, including two attack transports that went down immediately, and two destroyers that followed within hours. Our former steaming partner, the ex-IJN cruiser *Sakawa* went down the next day.

Ex-IJN cruiser Sakawa immediately after the blast. Photo USN.

To many of us, the event was a bit of a disappointment. One of the pirate crew swore that the blast sounded like a wet firecracker.

Despite the towering plume, some of the 114 press observers expressed disappointment at the effect on the target ships. *The New York Times* reported that (prematurely, as it turned out) "only two were sunk, one capsized, and eighteen damaged."

Cover-your-ass began immediately with SECNAV James Forrestal formulating the position that "heavily built and heavily armored ships are difficult to sink unless they sustain underwater damage." Dark rumors circulated that Navy had rigged the test to disadvantage proponents of a new, independent Air Force that would be established as a peer to the existing Departments of War and the Navy.

Actually, the reason for the SNAFU had no conspiracy, but equally no simple answers. *GILDA* had missed the aim-point of the battleship *Nevada*, by 710 yards. Meteorologists reported that high humidity in the lagoon absorbed much of the radiant light and heat energy.

Others speculated that the spectacle was minimized due to the fact that observers were prudently located much further away than they had been on the first atomic test at Trinity flats in New Mexico. The actual detonation point, west-northwest of *Nevada*, was closer to the attack transport USS *Gilliam* in an area with a much less dense aggregation of target ships.

The military did what it does best, and launched an immediate investigation of the aircrew of Dave's Dream. A variety of factors for the miss were offered up, including Gilda's known poor ballistic characteristics, but none was definitive. Images of the drop were inconclusive. The bombsight was checked and found to be calibrated properly and error free. Drops of the bomb simulators - the "pumpkins" were also held and checked out to be within tolerance.

Commander of the 509th, Col. Paul Tibbets, the man who had flown Enola Gay to Hiroshima opined the miss was caused by pilot and bombardier error. The smart money maintained that had the bomb exploded over the *Nevada* as planned, at least nine ships, including two battleships and an aircraft carrier, would likely have sunk.

Sakawa goes down by the stern the day after the ABLE test. In the center is *Nevada*, the ostensible target of the blast, while Nagato is in the upper right. Combat Art from LCDR Art Beaufort. Photo USN.

After a couple hours, scientists, technicians and Navy divers swarmed over the ships with Geiger counters, to assess damage, and some began to sweep down the ships to ameliorate the radiation. Other crews returned to the target ships to put out fires. *Nagato* floated placidly just where we left her, apparently inured to the power of the atom.

We waited a day, and then returned to our battleship in the target zone. We discovered that the ship was scorched, but otherwise intact. The long boat had been blown to bits, and the decks were scorched, but otherwise there was no damage. My stateroom had a quarter of inch of rust particles on the floor. Evidently the ship had shaken itself like a wet dog, and rust had spurted from every joint. Everything was mildly radioactive, but not enough to worry about. We lived on board just as before, preparing for the BAKER test, and I went back to the coral head to swim during the day.

The Moray Eel appeared to have survived the ABLE test just fine, though perhaps a bit more irritable.

DEMON CORE

Between swimming in the lagoon and supervising the Bo'sun there was enough to do. Boats began to order the deck department to commence dogging hatches and assisting the technicians place their sensors. The morning rains and the sultry afternoons made any time below decks or inside the armored citadel of the ship oppressive.

The things we did not know about the Atomic Age were legion, and we would soon be finding out some more.

Idle hands are the devil's workshop, and people got to talking about things that, strictly speaking, we didn't have a need to know. One afternoon I struck up a conversation with one of the techs in my office in Ship's Admin. He was aboard to place some special motion sensors with needles that would record the impact of the Test BAKER base surge on *Nagato's* hull.

It turned out he was a mid-grade member of the engineering team from Los Alamos. That is where the bombs were assembled after the fissile material arrived from the Hanford Nuclear Reservation in Oregon. I offered him some Navy coffee that we made with water distilled from the water in the atoll and he accepted gratefully.

He put his feet up on my metal desk and slumped into the Navy-issue straight backed chair. He then proceeded to tell me an amazing story.

Apparently the A-Bomb we called "GILDA" was powered by something called The Demon Pit, which was so lethal that it had already killed two physicists working on the Manhattan District Engineering Project.

Apparently there was very little of the "plutonium" material that was used to make the core of the bombs. GILDA was only the fourth one ever manufactured, and only the second of the "Fat Man" design, one of which was used against Nagasaki.

The experiments that were conducted at Los Alamos were designed to guarantee that the "core" was indeed close to the critical point by arranging reflectors around them and seeing how much (or how little) neutron reflection was required to approach super-criticality- the place where things go "boom," like GILDA had done just a few days before.

A re-creation of the experiment during which the 1946 accident occurred. The halfsphere is seen but the core inside is not. The beryllium hemisphere is held up with a screwdriver. Photo AEC.

It was a marvel to me as an engineer that something that small- six or seven pounds- could produce an explosion equal to that of tens of thousands of tons of TNT.

On August 21, 1945, the plutonium core that would become GILDA produced a burst of radiation that killed a physicist named Harry Daghlian. Apparently he was working alone in the lab with the core, performing experiments on the reflector arrays that would surround it.

Harry was placing a stack of neutron-reflective tungsten carbide bricks around the core. Each time he moved one of them he was also moving a step closer to making the core go critical. While attempting to stack an additional brick around the assembly, Harry accidentally dropped it onto the core, causing it to go well into super-criticality, which is a self-sustaining critical chain reaction. He lunged forward and grabbed the brick off the assembly but it was too late. In less than a second Harry had received a fatal dose of radiation. He died 25 days later from acute radiation poisoning.

GILDA's core was lethal and would soon kill again. On May 21, 1946, a physicist named Louis Slotin and seven other Los Alamos personnel were in a laboratory conducting another experiment to verify the exact point at which the core of fissile material could be made critical by positioning neutron reflectors around it.

Slotin was demonstrating the technique to another physicist, since he was going to use it in the ABLE Test here at Bikini. Despite the heat and humidity, I felt the hairs stand up on my arms as I listened to the scientist describe the scene.

This is about the most expensive and secret program in the history of mankind, after all and it all seemed a bit casual. The Scientist continued:

"See, the trick is that you place two half-spheres of beryllium around the core to block the neutrons. You then lower the top reflector over the core by a thumb hole on the top, sort of like a bowling ball."

"The bowling ball from hell," I said.

"Exactly. Allowing the two reflectors to close completely

could result in the instantaneous formation of a critical mass and a lethal release of radiation. The way Louie would do it, he would take the blade of a screwdriver and keep it between the edges of the two hemispheres.

"He was pretty cocky about his technique and was the local expert we turned to when we tried to calibrate the things." He sipped his Navy coffee and grimaced. It is strong stuff, intended to keep watch-standers awake.

"The only thing preventing the core from going super-critical was the blade of a standard straight screwdriver and Slotin's ability to keep it twisted just enough.

"He must have done it a dozen times, wearing just his signature blue jeans and cowboy boots. He did it once in front of the greatest Atomic scientist in the world, Enrico Fermi, who was not impressed."

"What did he say?" I asked, wishing there was a cold Coca Cola on the ship, or maybe just a tot of the grain alcohol the pirate crew had found and never shared with the officers.

"Fermi said Slotin would be dead within the year. And he was right. On the day of the accident, Slotin's screwdriver slipped outward a fraction of an inch while he was lowering the top reflector, which allowed the reflector to fall into place around the core. There was an intense flash of blue light and a wave of heat rolled across Slotin's skin as the core released an intense burst of neutron radiation."

"It was over in less than a second, but the damage was done. His body shielded the others in the lab at the time, but he received a lethal dose of gamma rays in under a second and died nine days later. The guy he was teaching was partially exposed and also got a severe dose but eventually recovered."

"This is amazing information," I said. "This plutonium stuff sounds kind of frightening."

GILDA, the 23-kiloton air-deployed nuclear weapon using the "demon core," detonated on July 1, 1946 during Test ABLE. Photo USN.

"It did to the people at Los Alamos as well. After that, the plutonium intended for the Fat Man bombs were referred to as the 'demon cores.' Hands-on experiments were forbidden and remote-control machines were designed by one of the survivors, to perform the experiments. All personnel were directed to remain a quarter-mile away from the laboratory."

"You bet. I don't think we really understand what we are dealing with here, but we needed to get it ready and use it to stop the war. Otherwise, a lot more people would have died."

"I imagine so. Do you really think the people on Joint Task

Force ONE understand all the ins and outs of this radiation business?"

"Of course. We have the best scientists in the world on this."

"That is a relief. Two more tests to go here at Bikini and we can all go home."

"Amen to that. But I suspect there is going to be a lot more of this atomic stuff in the days ahead."

THE FABULOUS BAKER BOYS

LSM-60 configured for the BAKER test. Shown here is the antenna used to receive the radio signal that would trigger the bomb. The mid-ship hoist used to lower the bomb to the caisson is shown just forward of the bridge. This was the first underwater test of an atomic device, and the explosion produced so many unusual phenomena that a conference was held two months later to define new terms for use in descriptions and analysis. Photo USN.

Preparations continued in the lagoon throughout the first weeks of July, 1946, for the second Atomic test of the three-blast series of demonstrations. This one was imaginatively termed "BAKER." People were constantly coming and going from *Nagato's* deck as we pumped her out and dogged down hatches. Technicians were placing curious pie-plates with holes drilled in them to evaluate the effect of the atomic rays passing on shielded and unshielded surfaces.

Surveys of structural and watertight integrity, installation of test equipment, stripping of armament and other items not required as test equipment were conducted. The target ships were loaded as closely as possible to the battle or operating displacement of the ships. Varying percentages of the wartime allowance of ammunition and of the normal capacity of fuel oil and gasoline were carried in the ships' magazines and bunker tanks.

In some cases, emergency repairs were made to correct damage caused by the ABLE tests.

There wasn't much talk about the SNAFU that had caused the ABLE Day bomb to land so far from the intended target. Joint Task Force ONE was configuring the test ship for the shallow-water detonation. *ABLE* had been an airburst, and the scientists told us this was high enough above the surface to prevent materials being drawn up into the fireball. My friend from Los Alamos told me the height-of-burst for the first nuclear explosion at Trinity Flats had been on a tower about a hundred feet high. It produced a crater 6 feet deep and 500 feet wide, and there was some local radioactive material in the air- what he termed a new thing called "Fallout."

We knew nothing about anything like that at the time-Trinity had been a secret test, after all, and the two bombs used on Japan had been detonated at altitude. We were assured everything was accounted for, and we trusted them. They were the experts, after all.

ABLE had been set to go off at 520 feet, an altitude considered to be sufficient that the radioactive products would rise to the stratosphere and become part of the global environment rather than contaminating the local area. The scientists knowingly told us that the airburst was considered to "self-cleansing," which is why we were permitted to re-embark the battleship so quickly.

That was not going to be the case for the BAKER test. To get a better feel for the effects of the concussion and blast on surface ships and submarines, the Fat Man bomb was slung in a caisson at a depth of 90 feet below a medium sized landing vessel. LSM- 60 was anchored in the exact middle of the target formation, and thus was prepared to become the first ship ever to deploy an A-Bomb.

This device, by the way, also had a name, just as "GILDA" did. The BAKER bomb was named "Helen of Bikini." I never got a decent explanation for why they chose that name, since Helen of Troy was the cause of the Trojan Wars. Perhaps like naming hurricanes after women, the fury of the devices was supposed to be akin to that sometimes displayed by the fairer sex.

In preparation, there was swimming, and last visits to the Officers Club that had been established ashore- the "Up and Atom."

As the test date approached, "Helen of Bikini," was placed in a steel caisson manufactured by the scientists at Los Alamos from the conning tower of USS *Salmon* (SS-182) that had been scrapped in April 1946. Carl Hatch, U.S. Senator from New Mexico and an observer at the tests, chalked the words "Made in New Mexico" on its side before it was lowered down.

ᴿᴾ989-7/23-BIKINI-Battening down the hatches aboard the battleship Nagato are W.H.Brown,S2/c of Gastonia,N.C. (left) and H.L. Robinson, machinist's mate 3/c, of Rockport,Mass.,as final preparations are being made for test Baker.Joint Army-Navy Task Force One photo.ACME TELEPHOTO

The test was set for the 25th of July- the 24th on the other side of the Dateline back stateside, and we followed the same drill as we did for the ABLE test. We ensured that *Nagato* was as ready as she was going to be, hatches dogged tight, pie pans set, instruments placed, and all made ready. We had no test animals onboard, but other ships did- pigs and rats this time. All the goats had been offered up to ABLE.

Then we were again evacuated to the support ships anchored this time nearly nineteen miles away from the point of detonation. We had a movie night and ice cream that melted rapidly. I slept well, though not in my own bunk on the Japanese battleship where things made a sort of surreal sense.

BAKER in the morning.

AT THE CROSSROADS

Nagato seemed all right after the Baker blast, though the Radiological Control officers told us it was unsafe to go aboard. We circled her in the landing craft, and it was hard to believe that our erstwhile home was now emitting dangerous radiation. She appeared a little lower in the water, as if some seams had been opened, and I suspected she was taking on water.

There was nothing that could be done, since we could not activate the pumps nor perform even the most routine damage control. She sank lower in the water every day as the VADM Blandy's experts tried to figure out what to do about salvaging the ships still afloat for the CHARLIE Test.

Some ships, less radioactive than ours were boarded and

attempts were made to hose them down. Our pirate crew was parceled out for the clean-up of the fleet, and we never came together as a crew again.

By the morning of the 30th *Nagato* was gone. No one saw her go, but she had been there at taps on the evening of the 28th and by morning she wasn't there. Combat Artist Grant Powell depicted the moment she groaned and gave it up to the deep:

By July 30, many target ships remained too radioactive for boarding, and it was becoming apparent that the target fleet was much more heavily contaminated than had been expected. For all but 12 target vessels, the target fleet remained too contaminated to allow more than brief onboard activities. Most of the thorough inspection and documentation of BAKER's effects, a primary objective of Operation CROSSROADS, was seriously delayed.

Within a week after the detonation, the JTF staff realized that they had to attempt to decontaminate the target vessels, even though the radiation on the targets was completely unexpected, no plans had been prepared for organized decontamination measures.

Beginning on August 1, the morning the battleship had taken her leave, work crews drawn from the target ships companies sprayed and scrubbed the ships exteriors.

Initially, decontamination proceeded slowly because "safe time" aboard some of the target ships was severely limited, sometimes to only a few minutes. Also, removing the radioactive particles imbedded in the paint, rust, and organic materials of the ships was a very slow and labor-intensive process.

Crews experimented with a variety of techniques and

decontaminating agents – including blasting with ground co-conut shells, rice, ground coffee, and sand – but none worked well enough to significantly speed up the process.

Radioactive contaminants had spread to the lagoon anchorage of the support fleet. This became a serious problem as contamination accumulated in the ships' evaporators, saltwater piping, and marine growth on the outside of their hulls, potentially exposing shipboard personnel to low-level radiation.

We worked each day with whatever task the Joint Task Force decided we could manage. It was hot. The sailors mostly were in shorts and worked shirtless. While many of them were issued "dosimeter" badges to record the amount of radioactive exposure they had received, most of us did not.

The priority for issuance was to individuals thought to be at the greatest risk for radiological contamination along with a percentage of each group who were working in less contaminated areas. Personnel were removed for one or more days from areas and activities of possible exposure if their badges showed more than "0.1 roentgens (R)" per day exposure.

They told us that measurement of ionization produced in air by X-Rays or gamma radiation was a good means of assessing exposure to other things, like plutonium from the BAKER core that could not be measured.

They told us at the time that this radiation dose could be tolerated by individuals for long periods without any harmful effects., and there was never any record of what we had dealt with. On the *Mount McKinley*, there were apparently some tense moments between Admiral Blandy and Dr. Stafford Warren, the Army Colonel in charge of the radiation safety program. He had been Chief of the Manhattan Project's medical section and was the only person in a position to take on the Admiral about safety matters. At Operation Crossroads, it was his job to keep the sailors safe during the cleanup, and to avoid giving them grounds to sue the Navy if health problems developed later.

There did not seem to be a viable cleanup plan. Nobody expected that almost the entire target fleet would be bathed in radioactive water, and no decontamination procedures had been tested in advance to see if they would work. The sailors were set to work using traditional deck-scrubbing methods: hoses, mops, and brushes, with water, soap, and lye.

Unprotected sailors were stirring up radioactive material and contaminating their skin, clothing, and, presumably, their lungs. When they returned to their support ship living quarters, they contaminated the shower stalls, laundry facilities, and everything they touched.

By August 3, Colonel Warren concluded the entire effort was futile and dangerous, and demanded an immediate halt to the entire cleanup operation.

Blandy disagreed. From what I was told on the trip home, the Admiral did not know that there was no way to detect plutonium, which could have been anywhere. The plan had been to decontaminate the ships and sail them home in triumph after the CHARLIE Test the next year.

It took a week to convince the Admiral. The immediate

public relations problem was to avoid any perception that the entire target fleet had been destroyed. On August 6, in anticipation of this development, Blandy had told his staff that ships sunk or destroyed more than 30 days after the *Baker* shot "will not be considered as sunk by the bomb." By then, public interest in Operation Crossroads was waning, and the reporters had gone home. The failure of decontamination did not make news until the final reports came out a year later, when we were all home again.

It seemed we had a lot to learn about the atomic age.

CROSSROADS was over.

Vice Admiral Spike Blandy and his wife cut a mushroom cloud cake, while Admiral Frank J. Lowry looks on at a reception after returning to the States in November 1946. It is not a coincidence about Mrs. Blandy's hat.

FUBAR

Deck Department conducting decontamination drill on one of the support ships after the BAKER Test at Bikini Atoll. Photo USN.

T here is a corollary to the term "SNAFU." It is "FUBAR," which is usually the end-state of a SNAFU that goes beyond the normal regime. That was precisely the situation in the lagoon at Bikini after the BAKER blast.

Sailors sent aboard the target ships were exposed to radiation as they tried to decontaminate them. They in turn brought radiation back to the support fleet, and through it all, we were taking seawater in from the lagoon to distill and use for cooking, coffee, laundry and showers.

All the pigs and most of the rats on the test ships died, though it was several days before sailors were able to re-board the target ships where test animals were located; during that time the accumulated doses from the gamma rays produced by fission products became lethal for the animals. The reporters and correspondents were gone by that time. Much of the public interest in Operation CROSSROADS had focused on the fate of the test animals, so by September Vice Admiral Blandy issued a press release stating that the tests had demonstrated that radiation death is not painful. "The animal merely languishes and recovers or dies a painless death," he said. "Suffering among the animals as a whole was negligible."

I was dubious about that. The scientist from Los Alamos I had befriended on *Nagato* had been graphic about the suffering of his two associates who had been killed by exposure to the Demon Core, but that was not a matter of public knowledge. Privately, the consensus was that if the target ships had been fully manned at the time of the tests, there would have been 35,000 casualties.

After the August 10 decision to stop decontamination work at Bikini, the surviving target fleet was towed to Kwajalein Atoll where the live ammunition and fuel could be offloaded in uncontaminated water, thereby contaminating it. That was a more normal sort of SNAFU than what had happened in the aftermath of the BAKER shot. Most of the personnel were embarked in support ships, and transported back to CONUS. By September, only a residual force of some working parties was left to try to clean up the facilities ashore.

Transmitter final tuning capacitor from the WWII Japanese Battleship *Nagato*. Image courtesy Antique Wireless Association, Bloomfield, New York.

Nagato and *Sakawa* were at the bottom of the lagoon and were going to stay there. Eight of the major ships and two submarines were towed back to the United States and Hawaii for radiological inspection. Twelve target ships were so lightly contaminated that they were re-manned and sailed back to the United States by their original crews. The support ships were decontaminated as necessary and received a radiological clearance before they could return to the Fleet. We could have told them the answer about decontamination efforts- they don't work.

The hulls of the support ships that entered the lagoon after BAKER became so radioactive that sleeping quarters were moved toward the center of each ship. All the support ships that returned to the lagoon were to some degree radiologically suspect, depending on how long they spent near ground zero and how much water from the lagoon they had processed through their pipes and tanks.

I was assigned to get a ride home on the USS *Rockwall* (APA-230), a *Haskell*-class attack transport. As we made preparations to get underway for the TRANSPAC, I saw what the working parties were asked to do. Some sailors swabbed the decks, while others were lowered to the water in dinghies, given short-handled hoes and told to start scraping. As the gentle waves jostled the ships, the men would be thrown against the hull, encrusted with the green algae slime and barnacles, painting their sweating torsos with the contaminated organic material.

A couple members of *Rockwall's* deck department lost their hair, and sported bald pates until a new crop of hair grew in.

Accommodations were Spartan, but at the end of it was San Francisco, and home. I passed the time making some rough notes about what I had seen in Japan and the technical characteristics of Japanese naval architecture and ship design. When we got back to San Francisco, some of the CROSSROADS ships were directed to fly the yellow pennant signifying "quarantine" until shore authorities were satisfied they were no threat.

As a practical matter, that meant cleaning surfaces and flushing systems with caustic solutions, dismantling the water intakes and boiler operating systems. Hundreds of rags were used, and then discarded overboard.

As an officer, I did not have to take part in that, but I was happy to grab my seabag and disembark in Oakland and take the train back across the country to Washington to make a final report to the Technical Assessment Team - Japan before I could be demobilized the following January and return to civilian life.

As part of out-processing at the Washington Navy Yard, I was cautioned that the events I had experienced at Bikini were considered restricted data, and that I should not talk about it.

The return to civilian life was preceded by a cursory physical examination. Then I was thanked for my service, and handed the coveted Ruptured Duck pin for my lapel, signifying my honorable discharge from the Navy.

I am only telling you this because I am not sure that anyone else is going to be around to tell the story of the last cruise of the battleship *Nagato*.

I have had a series of skin problems over the years, possibly because I have spent a lot of time in the sun while diving, and some other nagging problems. But I just received a diagnosis saying I have something called "multiple myeloma."

The prognosis is not good, they tell me. This account is something I have been meaning to get to for several years, and it is as good as I can give at this remove from the events. I also need to find a home for the vacuum tubes and condenser I removed from the battleship as well. They are historic and were part of the radio that announced the Japanese attack to Admiral Yamamoto on Pearl Harbor thirty-six years ago this month.

Someone may be interested someday.

Edward Smith Gilfillen
Saratoga, New York
December, 1977

EPILOGUE

Ed Gilfillen passed from this world in 1978, and after his death his wife managed to get the radio tubes of the Last Battleship to my uncle, who in turn delivered them to the Antique Wireless Museum: 6925 NY-5, Bloomfield, NY 14469.

I have written the Museum to ensure that they are aware of the provenance of the artifacts in their care.

RADM Mac Showers donated the small battle flag of *Nagato* (it is still pretty large) to the Office of Naval Intelligence in 2012 in an impressive small ceremony just months before his death. You can see it if you can get past security at ONI's Suitland, MD, Headquarters.

The details of the last cruise are contained in a double-spaced manuscript written by CDR Gilfillen. I have taken some small liberties in the interest of clarity, and elaborated on some nautical terms. Since the Xeroxed copy is of marginal quality, there may be errors not originally penned by the original author. While the cruise is detailed meticulously, there is only cursory reference to the time in Eniwetok for repairs (except for the snorkeling) and virtually nothing about *Nagato's* role in the ABLE and BAKER tests in Operation Crossroads. I have reconstructed these events from available original sources.

Most of the Atomic Veterans were instructed to treat their experiences as classified, and in view of the significant number of radiation-related illnesses, I have a suspicion that Ed was reluctant to share his recollection of the two Atomic tests in which *Nagato* participated. I am confident that had radiation contamination not precluded Ed's Deck Division from returning to the ship, she would have stayed afloat.

The exposure of thousands of the 42,000 personnel present for the tests was a matter of controversy which continues to this day, though most of the 1946-era veterans have now passed away.

There is no total of the number whose deaths were hastened by exposure to radiation, largely from the BAKER underwater explosion. A review of the matter was initiated in 1994, by former President Bill Clinton, who apologized to the Veterans for their treatment in 1995. A year later, Congress repealed the Nuclear Radiation Secrecy Agreement Act, which rescinded the oath of secrecy imposed on service members who participated in the Atomic testing cycle, and gave those still living the opportunity to recount their stories without legal penalty.

By that time, however, many thousands of the veterans, like Ed Gilfillen, had succumbed to a host of radiation-related health issues, and had taken their secrets with them to Fleet Landing on the other side of the Styx. This was an attempt to give his voice an opportunity to be heard, finally.

Nagato herself is exactly where she was during the BAKER

test, though capsized, as is depicted in this US Park Service sketch:

Her distinctive pagoda superstructure is snapped off, and lies nearby in 180 feet of clear water. As hard as her armor plate might be, wrecks are finite things, and will not be around forever.

Nagato can be visited, should you be a competent sport diver. A link to a recent YouTube video of a dive may be sufficient:

https://www.youtube.com/watch?v=PdYw_ahP5pY

If you feel a compulsion to swim where Ed Gilfillen and Admiral Yamamoto walked, contact the Bikini Atoll Dive Tourism and reservation information: tbikiniatolldivers@gmail.com.

Their season runs from late April to November, at this time Bikini Atoll is not open from December through early April. The access portal in the Marshall Islands is at Kwajalein Atoll, which can be reached by United Airlines, though there are no direct flight from CONUS. Travel from Kwajalein to Bikini is by boat. The M/V *Windward* covers the open ocean 215 nautical miles in about 18 hours, with sheltered water for about seven. The entire trip takes about 25 hours depending on sea conditions and current. Reservations and suitable equipment are a must.

SHIP DISPOSITION

THE DISPOSITION OF ALL the target ships is as follows, compiled by Capt. A. G. Nelson, USN, in a memorandum for the Department of Energy entitled "Crossroads Target Ships," dated May 25, 1978, DOE/CIC 48703.

CARRIERS

Independence (CVL-22): Towed to Pearl Harbor and then to Hunters Point (San Francisco) in October 1946. Sunk as target in special tests of new aerial and undersea weapons off San Francisco on January 27, 1951, in 1,000 fathoms.

Saratoga (CV-3): Sunk at Bikini by BAKER shot on July 25, *1946.*

BATTLESHIPS

Arkansas (BB-33): Sunk at Bikini by BAKER shot on July 2S, 1946.

Nagato (Japanese): Sunk at Bikini by BAKER shot on night of July 29/30, *1946.*

Nevada (BB-36): Towed to Kwajalein by USS *Preserver (ARS-8),* decommissioned on August 29, 1946, and then towed to Pearl Harbor. Sunk as target on July 31, 1948, 65 miles southwest of Pearl Harbor following four days of gunfire, bomb, rocket, and torpedo hits from Task Force 12. As of 1993, the USS *Preserver* was still on active duty as a salvage ship, assigned to the Naval Reserve Training Facility at Little Creek outside Norfolk.

New York (BB-34): Towed to Kwajalein by USS *Achomawi (AFT-148)*, decommissioned on August 29, 1946, and then towed to Pearl Harbor. Sunk as target on July 8, 1948, 40 miles southwest of Pearl Harbor after an eight-hour pounding by ships and planes using bombs and gunfire in full-scale battle maneuvers with new torpedoes.

Pennsylvania (BB-38): Scuttled off Kwajalein on February 10, 1948.

CRUISERS

Pensacola (CA-23): Towed to Kwajalein and then to Bremerton, Washington, for radiological tests. Sunk as target off Washington coast on November 10, 1948, in 1,400 fathoms.

Prinz Eugen (German): Towed to Kwajalein and attempted to beach at Enubuj Island, but she capsized and sank in shallow water on December 22, 1946 *(New York Times* article indicates date was December 16).

Sakawa (Japanese): Sunk at Bikini by ABLE shot on July 2, 1946.

Salt Lake City (CA-25): Towed to Bremerton via Pearl Harbor for radiological tests. Sunk by torpedoes in 2,000 fathoms off San Diego on May 25, 1948, after a four-hour bombardment from planes and ships.

DESTROYERS

Anderson (DD-41 1): Sunk at Bikini by ABLE shot on July 1, 1946.

Conyngham (DD-371): Steamed from Kwajalein to Pearl Harbor in September 1946, and then to San Francisco area, arriving on October 22, 1946. Scuttled in July 1948 off California coast.

Hughes (DD-410): Beached at Eneu Island following BAKER shot on July 26, 1946, and later towed to San Francisco for radiological tests. Sunk as target off Washington coast by air attack on October 16, 1948.

Lamson (DD-367): Sunk at Bikini by ABLE shot on July 1, 1946.

Mayrant (DD-402): Kept at Kwajalein for radiological tests until sunk there by guns and torpedoes on April 4, 1948.

Mugford (DD-389): Scuttled off Kwajalein on March 22,1948.

Mustin (DD-413): Sunk by gunfire off Kwajalein on April 18, 1948.

Ralph Talbot (DD-390): Scuttled off Kwajalein on March 8, 1948.

Rhind (DD-404): Scuttled off Kwajalein on March 22, 1948.

Stack (DD-406): Sunk by gunfire from four destroyers off Kwajalein on April 24, 1948.

Trippe (DD-403): Sunk as target off Kwa'alein on February 3, 1948.

Wainwright (DD-419): Sunk as target off Kwajalein on July S, 1948, by Destroyer Division 172.

Wilson (DD-408): Scuttled off Kwa'alein on March 8, 1948.

SUBMARINES

Apogon (SS-308): Sunk at Bikini by BAKER shot on July 25, 1946.

Dentuda (SS-335): Steamed from Kwajalein to Pearl Harbor

in September 1946, and the next month to San Francisco for radiological study.

Decommissioned at Mare Island on December 11, 1946, and stationed in the 12th Naval District for training of naval reservists. Sold for scrap on January 20, 1969.

Parche (SS-384): Steamed to Pearl Harbor and then reported to Mare Islands Group 19th Fleet on October 14, 1946. Towed to the naval reserve docks in Oakland in February 1948 and accepted as a naval reserve training ship. Sold for scrap in July 1970.

Pilotfish (SS-386): Sunk at Bikini by BAKER shot on July 25, 1946. Salvaged for examination and resunk as a target on October 16, 1948. *Searaven* (SS-196): Raised from submerged position on July 29, 1946, after BAKER shot. Steamed to Pearl Harbor from Kwajalein and then to San Francisco for radiological study, arriving there on October 22, 1946. Sunk as target off California coast on September 11, 1948.

Skate (SS-305): Towed to Kwajalein by ATR-40, then to Pearl Harbor by USS *Fulton* (AS-11), and then to San Francisco by USS

Clamp (ARS-33). Decommissioned on December 11, 1946, and scuttled off California coast in 515 fathoms on October 4, 1948.

Skipjack (SS-184): Sunk at Bikini by BAKER shot on July 25, 1946. Salvaged on September 2, towed to Pearl Harbor, and then to San Francisco. Sunk by aircraft rocket attack on August 11, 1948, off California coast in 700 fathoms.

Tuna (SS-203): Surfaced after BAKER shot on July 27, 1946. Steamed to Kwa'alein, Pearl Harbor, and then San Francisco. Scuttled off the West Coast on September 24, 1948, in 1,160 fathoms.

ATTACK TRANSPORTS

Banner (APA-60): Scuttled off Kwajalein on February 16, 1948.

Barrow (APA-61): Scuttled off Kwajalein on May 11, 1948.

Bladen (APA-63): Steamed to East Coast, decommissioned at Norfolk on December 26, 1946, and transferred to U.S. Maritime Commission on August 3, 1953.

Bracken (APA-64): Scuttled off Kwajalein on March 10, 1948.

Briscoe (APA-65): Scuttled somewhere in the Marshall Islands on May 6, 1948.

Brule (APA-66): Scuttled off Kwajalein on May 11, 1948.

Butte (APA-68): Scuttled off Kwajalein on May 12, 1948.

Carlisle (APA-69): Sunk at Bikini by ABLE shot on July 1, 1946.

Carteret (APA-70): Sunk in the Marshall Islands by gunfire of the USS *Toledo* (CA-133) on April 19, 1948.

Catron (APA-71): Sunk in the Marshall Islands by gunfire of the USS *Atlanta* (CL-104) on May 6, 1948.

Cortland (APA-75): Granted radiological clearance in December 1946, decommissioned at Norfolk on December 30, 1946, and transferred to the U.S. Maritime Commission on March 31, 1948. Later sold for scrap.

Crittenden (APA-77): Towed to San Francisco in January 1947. Towed to sea by USS *Tekesta* (ATF-93) and sunk off California coast by explosive tests on October 5, 1948, in 800 fathoms.

Dawson (APA-79): Scuttled off Kwajalein on April 19, 1948, in 2,290 fathoms.

Fallon (APA-81): Beached on Eneu Island on July 27, 1946,

after BAKER shot and then towed to Kwajalein. Scuttled off Kwajalein on -March 10, 1948.

Fillmore (APA-83): Steamed to East Coast, decommissioned at Norfolk on January 24, 1947, and transferred to U.S. Maritime Commission on April 1, 1948.

Gasconade (APA-85): Towed to San Francisco and sunk as target by torpedoes off southern California coast on July 21, 1948, in 1,300 fathoms.

Geneva (APA-86): Steamed to East Coast, decommissioned at Norfolk on

January 1, 1947, and received by the U.S. Maritime Commission at James River Reserve Fleet, Lee Hall, Virginia, on April 2, 1948. Transferred to Wilmington (North Carolina) Reserve Fleet in July 1955, and sold for scrap on November 2, 1966.

Gilliam (APA-57): Sunk at Bikini by ABLE shot on July 1, 1946.

Niagara (APA-87): Steamed to East Coast, arriving at Norfolk on November 23, 1946. After being used to test effects of special conventional explosives in the Chesapeake Bay in 1947-48, was sold for scrap on February 5, 1950, to Northern Metals Company of Philadelphia.

LSTs (LANDING SHIPS, TANK)

LST-S2: Sunk off Kwajalein in April 1948 by gunfire of USS Oakland (CL-95) in 2,280 fathoms.

LST-12S: Deliberately beached before BAKER shot, then sunk by gunfire of USS Fall River (CA- 1 3 1) off Bikini on August 14, 1946.

LST-133: Sunk off Kwajalein on May 11, 1948.

LST-220: Sunk off Kwajalein on May 12, 1948.

LST-545: Sunk off Kwajalein on May 12, 1948. LST-661: Sunk off Kwajalein on July 25, 1948.

LSMs (LANDING SHIPS, MEDIUM)

LSM-60: Destroyed at Bikini as bomb carrier for BAKER shot on July 25, 1946.

LCTs (LANDING CRAFT, TANK)

LCT-412: Scuttled off Kwajalein in September 1947.

LCT-414: Sunk by demolition charges at Bikini shortly after BAKER shot.

LCT-705: Scuttled off Kwa'alein in September 1947.

LCT-746: Scuttled off Kwajalein in March 1947.

LCT-812: Sunk by demolition charges at Bikini shortly after BAKER shot.

LCT-816: Scuttled off Kwajalein in June 1947.

LCT-818: Scuttled off Kwajalein in September 1947.

LCT-874: Scuttled off Kwajalein in September 1947.

LCT-1013: Scuttled off Kwajalein in September 1947.

LCT-1078: Scuttled off Kwajalein in September 1947.

LCT-1112: Scuttled off Kwajalein in September 1947.

LCT-1113: Scuttled off Kwajalein in June 1947.

L CT-1114: Capsized by BAKER shot and sunk by demolition charges at Bikini on July 30, 1946.

LCT-1175: Sunk at Bikini by BAKER shot on July 2S, 1946.

LCT-1187. Sunk by demolition charges at Bikini shortly after BAKER shot.

LCT-1237: Sunk by demolition charges at Bikini shortly after BAKER shot.

AUXILIARIES

ARDC-13: Sunk at Bikini by BAKER shot on
August 6, 1946.

YO-1 60: Sunk at Bikini by BAKER shot on July 25, 1946.

YOG-83: Beached at Kwajalein on September 23, 1946, and
scuttled off Kwajalein on September 16, 1948.

LCIs (LANDING CRAFT, INFANTRY)

LCI-327: Stranded at Bascombe (Mek) Island, Kwajalein,
and destroyed there on October 30, 1947.

LCI-329: Scuttled off Kwajalein on March 16, 1948.

LCI-332: Scuttled off Kwajalein in September 1947.

LCI-549: Used at Kwajalein as patrol vessel until June 1948.
Granted final radiological clearance in August 1948 and
towed to Port Chicago, California, in January 1949. Sold to
the Learner Company in Alameda, California, on August
2, 1949, and delivered on August 19, 1949.

LCI-618: Sold to the Learner Company in Alameda,
California, on August 2, 1949, and delivered on
August 19, 1949.

LCI-620: Deliberately beached before BAKER shot.
Towed to sea and sunk off entrance to Bikini lagoon on
August 10, 1946.

LCMs (LANDING CRAFT, MECHANIZED)

LCM-1: Fate unknown.

LCM-2: Fate unknown.

LCM-3: Fate unknown.

LCM-4: Sunk at Bikini by BAKER shot on July 25, 1946.

LCM-S: Fate unknown.

LCM-6: Sold for scrap in Guam on unknown date.

LCVPs (LANDING CRAFT VEHICLES, PERSONNEL)

LCVP-7: Fate unknown.

LCVP-8: Fate unknown.

LCVP-9: Fate unknown.

LCVP-1 0: Sunk at Bikini by BAKER shot on July 25, 1946.
LCVP-1 1: Fate unknown.

LCVP-12: Fate unknown.

AUTHOR BIO

Vɪᴄ Sᴏᴄᴏᴛʀᴀ is the pen name of J.R. Reddig, who has 27 years service as a Naval Intelligence Officer, and twenty more as an Intelligence Community insider. The pen-name was useful to keep his identity apart from his professional life, which started with the first detective novel written and printed on a commissioned Navy warship during the response to the Iranian seizure of the American embassy in Tehran. Like Ed's account of the Voyage to CROSSROADS, many of the tales he wanted to tell had to wait until the shrouds of secrecy were lifted. As editor of the Naval Intelligence Professionals organization, he became friends with some of the Old Salts who lived the history of how our institutions became what they are today. *Nagato*'s last voyage is one of them, and the time to tell them is now.